Macbeth

by William Shakespeare

Shelagh Hubbard

Series Editors:
Sue Bennett and Dave Stockwin

HODDER
EDUCATION
AN HACHETTE UK COMPANY

The publisher would like to thank the following for permission to reproduce copyright material:

Photo credits:

p. 9 Atlaspix/Alamy; **p. 11** TopFoto; **p. 15** dominic dibbs/Alamy; **p. 20** AF archive/Alamy; **p. 25** Everett Collection/Rex Features; **p. 41** TopFoto; **p. 44** Photostage

Although every effort has been made to ensure that website addresses are correct at time of going to press, Hodder Education cannot be held responsible for the content of any website mentioned. It is sometimes possible to find a relocated web page by typing in the address of the home page for a website in the URL window of your browser.

Orders: please contact Bookpoint Ltd, 130 Park Drive, Milton Park, Abingdon, Oxon OX14 4SE. Telephone: (44) 01235 827720. Fax: (44) 01235 400454. Lines are open 9.00–17.00, Monday to Saturday, with a 24-hour message answering service. Visit our website at www.hoddereducation.co.uk

© Shelagh Hubbard 2016

First published in 2016 by

Hodder Education

An Hachette UK Company,

Carmelite House, 50 Victoria Embankment

London EC4Y 0LS

Impression number	5	4	3	2	1
Year	2020	2019	2018	2017	2016

Cover photo © Photocreo Bednarek/Fotolia

Typeset in 11/13pt Bliss Light by Integra Software Services Pvt. Ltd., Pondicherry, India

Printed in Italy

A catalogue record for this title is available from the British Library

ISBN 9781471853623

Contents

Getting the most from this guide

This guide is designed to help you to raise your achievement in your examination response to *Macbeth*. You can use it throughout your GCSE English Literature course: it will help you when you are studying the play for the first time and also during your revision.

The following features have been used throughout this guide to help you focus your understanding of the play:

Target your thinking

A list of **introductory questions** labelled by Assessment Objective is provided at the beginning of each section to give you a breakdown of the material covered. They target your thinking in order to help you work more efficiently by focusing on the key messages.

Build critical skills

These boxes offer an opportunity to consider some **more challenging questions**. They are designed to encourage deeper thinking, analysis and exploratory thought. Building and practising critical skills in this way will give you a real advantage in the examination.

GRADE *FOCUS*

It is possible to know a play well and yet still underachieve in the examination if you are unsure of what the examiners are looking for. The **GRADE FOCUS** boxes give a clear explanation of how you may be assessed, with an emphasis on the criteria for gaining a Grade 5 and a Grade 8.

REVIEW YOUR LEARNING

At the end of each section you will find Review your learning questions to **test your knowledge**. These short questions will help you to check that you have understood and absorbed the key messages of the section. Answers to these questions are provided in the final section of the guide (on pp.109–112).

GRADE *BOOSTER*

Read and remember these pieces of helpful **grade-boosting advice**: top tips from experienced teachers and examiners who can advise you on what to do, as well as what not to do, to maximise your chances of success in the examination.

Key quotation

Key quotations are highlighted for you, so that if you wish you may use them as **supporting evidence** in your examination answers. Further quotations grouped by characterisation, key moments and theme can be found in the *Top ten* section (on pp. 102–106). Line references are given for the Cambridge School Shakespeare edition (ISBN 978-0-521-60686-8). '5.5 16–18' means 'Act 5 scene 5 lines 16–18'.

She should have died hereafter.

There would have been a time for such a word. –

Tomorrow, and tomorrow, and tomorrow…

(5.5 16–18)

Introduction

Studying the text

You may find it useful to read sections of this guide when you need them, rather than reading it from start to finish. For example, you can read the section on *Context* before you read the play itself, since it offers an explanation of relevant historical, cultural and literary background to the text. It is here where you will find information about aspects of Shakespeare's life and times which influenced his writing, the particular issues with which Shakespeare was concerned and where the play stands in terms of the literary tradition to which it belongs.

As you work through the play, you may find it helpful to read the *Plot and structure* section before or after reading a particular act or scene. As well as a summary of events there is also commentary, so that you are aware of both key events and features in each of the acts and scenes. The sections on *Characterisation*, *Themes* and *Language, style and analysis* will help to develop your thinking further, in preparation for written responses on particular aspects of the text.

Many students enjoy the experience of being able to bring something extra to their classroom lessons in order to be 'a step ahead of the game'. Alternatively, you may have missed a classroom session or feel that you need a clearer explanation and the guide can help you with this too.

An initial reading of the section on *Assessment Objectives and skills* will enable you to make really effective notes in preparation for assessments. The Assessment Objectives are what examination boards base their mark schemes on. In this section they are broken down and clearly explained.

Revising the text

Whether you study the play in a block of time close to the exam or much earlier in your GCSE English Literature course, you will need to revise thoroughly if you are to achieve the very best grade that you can.

You should first remind yourself of what happens in the play and so the section on *Plot and structure* might be the best starting point for revision. You might then look at the *Assessment Objectives and skills* section to ensure that you understand what the examiners are looking for in general, and then look carefully at *Tackling the exams*.

This section gives you useful information on question format, depending on which examination board specification you are following, as well as advice on the examination format and other practical considerations such as the time available for the question and the Assessment Objectives which apply to it. Advice is also supplied on how to approach the question, writing a quick plan, and 'working with' the text, since all of the examination boards offer an extract-based question for *Macbeth*.

Focused advice on how you might improve your grade follows, and you need to read this section carefully.

You will also find examples of exam-style responses in the *Sample essays* section, with examiner's comments in the margins, so that you can see clearly how to move towards a Grade 5 and then how to move from Grade 5 to Grade 8.

Now that all GCSE English Literature examinations are 'closed book', the *Top ten* section will be an invaluable aid, in that it offers you the opportunity to learn short quotations to support points about character and themes as well as a revision aid which identifies the top ten key moments in the downfall of Macbeth.

When writing about the play, use this guide as a springboard to develop your own ideas. Remember that the examiners are not looking for set responses so never try to memorise chunks of this guide to reproduce in the exam. Identical answers are dull. The examiners hope to reward you for perceptive thought, individual appreciation and varying interpretations. They want to sense that you have engaged with the themes and ideas in the play, explored Shakespeare's methods with an awareness of the context in which he wrote and enjoyed this part of your literature course.

The best way to enjoy Shakespeare is to see the play performed live in the theatre. However, if that is not possible, there are many film versions of *Macbeth*: in fact *Macbeth* is one of the most filmed of all Shakespeare's plays, though you will find interesting differences from the text in every film. For example, in *Macbeth on the Estate*, there are cars and guns and the characters are gangsters from Birmingham rather than Scottish soldiers. As far as the exam goes, films will not be a substitute for a detailed knowledge of the text itself. For example, examiners are unlikely to be impressed by responses which refer to car chases in Birmingham in *Macbeth*, or which describe the setting of the banquet scene as the local pub.

Enjoy referring to the guide as you study the text, and good luck in your exam.

Context

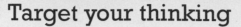

Target your thinking

- How much are historical events an influence on the play? (**AO3**)
- What moral and philosophical issues of this era does the play reflect? (**AO3**)
- Is the play still relevant to modern readers? (**AO3**)

The 'context' of a play means the circumstances in which it was written – the social, historical and literary factors that influenced what the author wrote, which also affect how audiences view the play at different times and in different places.

The social and historical context of *Macbeth* is important: Shakespeare's world was different from ours, more than four centuries later. Events unfolding during the playwright's lifetime and what he read himself influenced his writing. *Macbeth* was first performed around 1605 and appeared in various printed versions during the seventeenth century. It has been translated into every major language – and some less likely languages such as Setswana and Jamaican patois – and performed in theatres all over the world. It is one of Shakespeare's most popular works in countries as far apart as Russia, India and China.

William Shakespeare

The most important thing to know about Shakespeare's life is that he was a great playwright. However, reading what this section has to say about him and about the times and events of the world he lived in will help you make better sense of some of the historical and philosophical aspects of *Macbeth*.

William Shakespeare was born in Stratford-upon-Avon in 1564, the son of a prosperous merchant, and attended the local grammar school. He married Anne Hathaway when he was 18 and she was 26. They had three children: Susanna, born in 1583, and twins, Hamnet and Judith, in 1585.

Unlike most playwrights of his time, Shakespeare did not go to university, though he was obviously widely read and knowledgeable about events, developments and ideas.

Not much is known about his life before his plays became famous. Some say he was a teacher and there is a legendary tale that he was once arrested for poaching deer. When he moved to London in about 1590 he was already a playwright and an actor.

His plays

Shakespeare lived mainly in London for about 20 years and wrote most of his 37 plays there. Several of his plays may have been co-written with other playwrights or revised by other writers. It is not certain how many of his plays were actually written just by Shakespeare. The film *Shakespeare in Love* is a fictional reconstruction of what his life was like as he wrote *Romeo and Juliet* in the late 1500s.

His plays made him a wealthy man and he spent his money on property in his hometown of Stratford-upon-Avon. Shakespeare retired to Stratford in around 1610 and died there on 23 April 1616. He is buried in Stratford parish church where there is a famous bust of him.

Divine order

In the seventeenth century many people held the belief that God ordered all creation in a particular way. This was a medieval belief that would also have been held in the Scotland of the historical Macbeth. Everything on earth was considered part of a divine hierarchy with God at the top and all else ranked in a defined order below. God elected representatives to rule on earth: church leaders such as the pope or archbishops, and heads of state such as kings or emperors.

▲ The 'Chandos Portrait' of William Shakespeare, painted around 1610.

England at this time was a primarily Christian society and all but the most educated and liberal thinkers believed that what happened to you was dictated by outside forces stronger than the individual person. Most people believed not just in God but also in fate, destiny, fortune (luck) and the existence of the devil and other supernatural forces. Debates took place at the highest levels of the church about the extent to which individuals had free will. These debates had played an important role in the European Renaissance movement in the fifteenth century and still raged in Shakespeare's day.

This is central to *Macbeth*. Macbeth can only be blamed for his downfall if he freely chooses to act in response to the witches' words. If it is his inescapable fate and he is destined to do as he does, less blame will attach to him. Shakespeare and other playwrights of his time were groundbreaking in questioning the degree to which we might be able to direct our own lives and it is because questions like this are timeless that these plays are still enjoyed today.

James I and witchcraft

James VI of Scotland became James I of England when he was given the English throne in 1603 following the death of Elizabeth I. He was Scottish and descended from Banquo's line.

James was not especially popular with the English. People felt that the country was in some trouble after Elizabeth's death. Elizabethan England was a Protestant country, but James had been brought up as a Catholic. (England had been at war with Spain and Catholics were mistrusted.)

James was obsessed with witches and wrote a book about them.

- He described them as having beards.
- He believed they had the power to control the weather and to affect crops and livestock, but not to kill people. He also believed they could fly.
- He believed they received these supernatural powers by trading their soul with the devil in exchange for a familiar spirit or demon, an animal such as a cat, a bird or a reptile.
- He suggested that water would reject witches, because of its association with Christian baptism. A favourite 'trial' for a witch was to throw her in water. If she sank, she was innocent, but, unfortunately, drowned. If she floated, she was guilty and was put to death, usually by hanging. During the late 1500s and early 1600s there was a peak in numbers of executions of 'convicted' witches in England.

Build critical skills

When you have read Act 1 scenes 1 and 3 and Act 4 scene 1, consider how much of James I's view of witches you can identify in Shakespeare's depiction of the witches in *Macbeth*.

James I and the divine right of kings

James I emphasised the divine right of kings, probably because he felt insecure in his position. This is the idea that God chooses the king directly and that man has no right to interfere with God's wishes – another idea Shakespeare reflects in *Macbeth*. When James came to the throne, he became Patron of Shakespeare's company of actors and they changed their name from The Lord Chamberlain's Men to The King's Men. Obviously Shakespeare set out to please the king with his plays.

▲ A 1613 woodcut showing a witch 'trial'.

Ghosts and Christian beliefs

Most people in Shakespeare's time held firm Christian beliefs – they believed in heaven, hell and ghosts. Although Catholicism was out of favour in England, there were many people who secretly upheld the Catholic faith. Some say that Shakespeare was a Catholic: there are certainly signs in his plays that he understood the Catholic perspective.

Protestants and Catholics had a different understanding of what a ghost was: Catholics believed that ghosts might return from purgatory if they were 'unquiet' about things that had happened in their lives. These ghosts were the actual spirits of the dead and they told the truth. Protestants, on the other hand, believed that ghosts were demons in disguise, assuming a human form in order to achieve a devilish purpose.

Jacobean England and medieval Scotland

The setting

Shakespeare set the play in ancient Scotland. However, note that the characters behave more like the nobility of the Jacobean London court than would have been likely in tribal eleventh-century Scotland. This

Build critical skills

When you are trying to reach your own conclusion about what Macbeth sees when Banquo's ghost appears, consider how the context of the contemporary Christian view of ghosts influences your thinking.

would have increased the play's appeal to the new king. In addition, this historical setting deflected accusations of making direct criticisms of the society of Shakespeare's day. The support of the monarch was crucial to the survival of the theatre at the time because, in spite of its huge popularity, there was also much opposition to it. Many Puritans believed it to be sinful. Furthermore, large audiences brought the risk of spreading the bubonic plague and theatres closed for lengthy periods of time during outbreaks of the disease in the late 1500s. They closed permanently in 1642 but would have been shut down sooner without the backing of the monarch.

Source material

Holinshed's Chronicles told tales of many of the historic kings of England and Scotland. Shakespeare seems to have combined details from two stories. One deals with King Duncan and Macbeth and includes information about Banquo and his son Fleance, the ancestors of the Stewart line, the family of James I. The historical King Macbeth ruled during the eleventh century, born about 1005 and killed in battle by Malcolm Canmore, the son of Duncan, in 1057. The other story is of King Duffe, who died about 80 years before the historical Macbeth, and this story includes descriptions of witchcraft and spells.

GRADE *FOCUS*

Grade 5

Students will be able to show that they are *aware* of context and can comment clearly on how it is reflected in the text.

Grade 8

Students will be able to *make sustained comments and detailed links* between the play and relevant contextual information. In other words, they will be able to demonstrate in some detail how information from this section of the guide helps them to understand and interpret Shakespeare's play.

REVIEW YOUR LEARNING

1 What is meant by the context of a play?
2 Did Shakespeare make up the story of *Macbeth*?
3 Name the king on the throne when Shakespeare wrote *Macbeth*.
4 What religious beliefs did most English people hold at that time?
5 Why does Shakespeare use Scotland as a setting?
6 From what you know so far, does the play seem relevant to audiences in modern Britain?

Answers on p. 109.

Plot and structure

Target your thinking

- What are the main events of the play? (**AO1**)
- How has Shakespeare structured the play? (**AO2**)

Act 1 scene 1

Shakespeare grabs the attention of the audience: three witches plan to 'meet again'. They talk about a battle: 'hurlyburly'. They mention a heath – a desolate setting – and darkness, 'fog' and 'filthy air'. The third witch names Macbeth, who they plan to meet.

The witches' words rhyme and have a noticeable rhythm, perhaps reflecting the idea of chanting a spell. They are called away by 'Graymalkin' and 'Paddock', names for a cat and a toad. For Shakespeare's audience, this would be a frightening scene: the animals are 'familiars', creatures given to witches by the devil. Immediately their evil is linked with Macbeth.

The **paradoxical** line 'Fair is foul, and foul is fair...' (1.1 12) introduces an important theme: nothing is what it seems – the natural order has been turned upside down (see *Themes* pp. 50–51).

The stage directions would have presented a challenge when the play was first staged: there would have been no set and no lighting, though sound effects of thunder and some sort of smoke to suggest mist might have created an eerie atmosphere.

Paradox: a statement of opposite or contradictory ideas, though the words also contain a truth.

Build critical skills

Can you find another line that has a similar paradoxical meaning?

Build critical skills

Should we take Macbeth at face value from the outset, as those on stage seem to, as a brave and fearless fighter? Or should we see him as a ruthless killer?

Build critical skills

Why does Shakespeare draw our attention to King Duncan being so far away from the fighting that he only hears what happens by reports from the battlefield? The mention of the Norwegian King, Sweno, reminds us that a king should be at the front line, leading his troops. Who has taken on this role in place of Duncan?

Act 1 scene 2

The battle mentioned by the witches is described. The atmosphere of active conflict and bloody violence contrasts with the static eeriness and evil of the witches. An injured soldier describes vividly to the king how the battle was evenly balanced between the two sides, until Macbeth made short work of the rebel Macdonwald, disembowelling and beheading him. This is our introduction to the man the witches plan to meet.

Macbeth and Banquo are described as turning the battlefield into 'another Golgotha' (1.2 40). This is a comparison with the site of Christ's crucifixion: the place of the skull.

The Thane of Ross concludes the account: Macbeth fought on to gain victory over the Norwegians and rebels, overcoming the traitorous Thane of Cawdor. He is compared to Mars, the god of war: 'Bellona's bridegroom' (1.2 54).

The scene concludes with Duncan announcing the execution of the Thane of Cawdor. Macbeth is to be given the title as a reward.

Act 1 scene 3

Two witches confirm their evil natures, gleefully describing how they have passed the time killing pigs and tormenting a sailor by raising storms, merely because his wife refused one of them a chestnut.

Hearing the drum signalling Macbeth's approach, they speak a spell, circling three times in each direction.

Build critical skills

Note that three is a number with magical significance, and that the witches refer to themselves as 'weird sisters'. The word 'weird' links with an old English word 'wyrd' which means 'able to predict the future'. Shakespeare combines this old meaning with the modern meaning of 'odd' and 'strange'. How do details like this contribute to our judgement of the witches?

Macbeth's first words reflect the witches' chant in Act 1 scene 1, suggesting a bond between them:

So foul and fair a day I have not seen.

(1.3 36)

'Fair' because the battle has been won, 'foul' because of the misty weather, or referring to death in battle. The audience is reminded that nothing is exactly what it seems. Macbeth is not receptive to this concept, even when Banquo warns him not to be taken in by the words of the witches. Banquo comments on the witches' ambiguous appearance: their 'skinny lips' and 'choppy finger[s]'. Though they resemble women, they have 'beards'.

▲ The witches from an amateur dramatic production of *Macbeth*.

What happens next is crucial to the way the plot develops. The first witch greets Macbeth by name. The second greets him as Thane of Cawdor, the title the audience is aware the king has given to him. The third witch predicts the future, saying that he will become king.

Banquo notes Macbeth's shocked reaction and asks if they can predict *his* future as well. They reply with paradoxical words, then tell him that, although he will not be king himself, his descendants will.

GRADE *BOOSTER*

As the witches disappear Macbeth demands to know more. His words:
> The Thane of Cawdor lives…and to be king
> Stands not within the prospect of belief,
> No more than to be Cawdor.
> (1.3 70-73)

offer an example of dramatic irony, since the audience knows that Cawdor is dead, and the title now belongs to Macbeth. Demonstrating awareness of such techniques will raise your grade.

Build critical skills

How does Banquo's warning foreshadow later events? Consider Macbeth's failure to see the trickery of the witches' prophecies in Act 4. How does this warning add to the audience's understanding of the motivations behind Macbeth's later actions?

Macbeth and Banquo's discussion about the predictions is interrupted by the arrival of Ross and Angus. Ross greets Macbeth with the title which is his reward for his bravery in battle:

He bade me…call thee thane of Cawdor…

(1.3 103)

Banquo and Macbeth react to the witches in contrasting ways: Banquo fears some kind of trickery, but Macbeth reflects on the way he might bring the prediction to fruition. His speech is an aside. He speaks the word 'murder' and a 'horrid image' in his head terrifies him. He ends saying he will leave the prediction to chance, taking no action to make it come true.

Act 1 scene 4

Back at court, King Duncan asks Malcolm if Cawdor has been executed. The king's comment that he trusted the man and was deceived by his appearance is ironic, given the present thoughts of Macbeth, whom Duncan greets as 'worthiest cousin'.

Irony continues as wordy courtly speeches are made: the king apologises for the inadequacy of the reward and Macbeth makes a promise of loyalty. Compare this with Banquo's brief, sincere reply when Duncan thanks him.

Duncan announces that his eldest son, Malcolm, is to be given the title Prince of Cumberland: heir to the throne. He then announces that he will visit Macbeth's castle at Inverness.

Build critical skills

Given that Scottish kings were elected, that Duncan has played no active part in the battle and that Malcolm was almost captured, how might Macbeth, the hero of the hour, be seen as a better choice for the new king?

This has an immediate impact on Macbeth, who hurries away to acquaint his wife with his good news, revealing his true thoughts in an aside. Malcolm is an obstacle in his way to the throne and he speaks of hiding 'black and deep desires', though concealing his thoughts effectively, since the king describes him as 'worthy Cawdor…full so valiant…a peerless kinsman'.

Act 1 scene 5

Lady Macbeth reads aloud from a letter which describes Macbeth's success in battle, his meeting with the witches and their promises. His ambition is clear: 'King that shalt be', as he addresses her as his 'dearest partner in greatness'. Shakespeare emphasises the closeness of their relationship by the way Macbeth confides in her. Her reaction to the letter shows how well she knows him.

Note the metaphor 'milk of human kindness'. Up to now, Macbeth has been associated with blood and death – manly associations. Milk is feminine – nourishing and life-giving.

Shakespeare presents Lady Macbeth as a highly ambiguous character: she is a loyal, loving wife who wants the best for her husband, but at the same time she is ruthless – her mind jumps straight to murder. She is manipulative and understands the power of persuasive words.

Build critical skills

Why does Shakespeare introduce Lady Macbeth here? If we had seen her and perceived her ambitious nature before seeing Macbeth, how might we have responded to both the characters? What links can be made between the witches and Lady Macbeth?

A messenger brings the news that the king is to stay that night, and Lady Macbeth speaks a **soliloquy** which explicitly connects her with the 'instruments of darkness'. The mention of 'the raven', a bird of ill omen, could be seen as a link with the witches' familiars. The spirits Lady Macbeth calls on to remove her feminine weakness are referred to as 'murd'ring ministers'. Remember that people believed that witches could not kill – they had to find agents to do that for them.

References to breasts, milk and blood indicate that Lady Macbeth fears that femininity stands in the way of evil-doing – yet she has just expressed her doubts about her husband in similar terms.

She concludes by calling on the dark of night, the 'smoke of hell', to conceal the deeds she plans, another link with the fog that accompanied the witches.

Her speech is interrupted by Macbeth's entrance, and she acts as she said she would, seducing him with words into putting her in charge of 'this night's great business'.

GRADE *BOOSTER*

Note how here and elsewhere Lady Macbeth and Macbeth use **euphemistic** terms to refer to their murderous plan. Interpreting language devices in this way gains marks.

Her advice to her husband is to:

...look like th'innocent flower,

But be the serpent under't.

(1.5 63–64)

Build critical skills

Read the speech carefully and find the lines which emphasise qualities of Macbeth's character which would prevent him from taking 'the nearest way' to the crown: his kindness, his moral outlook, his fear of the consequences of evil-doing.

Soliloquy: a speech spoken by a lone actor to the audience.

Key quotation

Come you spirits

That tend on mortal thoughts, unsex me here!

(1.5 38–39)

Euphemism: using milder or less direct words or phrases ('business', 'be provided for') in place of stronger words or phrases (e.g. 'murder', 'killing').

She reminds us of Duncan's comments about the difficulty of judging the character of a person from his face. This also echoes the story of the Garden of Eden, casting Lady Macbeth as the temptress, Eve, and suggesting that Macbeth becomes the devil by assuming the role of the hidden snake.

Act 1 scene 6

This short scene provides more evidence of King Duncan's goodness and gullibility. He continues to judge by appearance, commenting on the appealing situation of the castle. Banquo agrees, pointing out the presence of nesting house martins, which indicates that the air is healthy. Compare the irony of this with the raven Lady Macbeth called on to greet Duncan and the smoke of hell-fire she summoned to conceal her deeds.

Lady Macbeth continues to demonstrate her acting skills, praising and thanking the king for honouring them with his presence. He is completely taken in by her words.

Act 1 scene 7

GRADE *BOOSTER*

Aspects of the structure of the play are repeated: Macbeth provides a banquet for his sovereign as he plans to kill him and later in the play he holds a banquet in honour of Banquo, whom he entraps and has killed on the way there. Both scenes explore Macbeth's weakness and Lady Macbeth's strength and control. Comments like this show your understanding of the whole play and lead to high grades.

Key quotation

I have no spur

To prick the sides of my intent, but only

Vaulting ambition....

(1.7 25–27)

Macbeth speaks the first of his three soliloquies, and reveals his doubts about pursuing the plan to assassinate Duncan. Macbeth is motivated by ambition which proves to be his ruin.

Lady Macbeth, furious to find her husband neglecting his guest and causing suspicion by not being a good host, becomes even more furious when he tells her he is not prepared to go through with the plan. She unleashes a tirade of insults against his lack of courage and his manhood. Finally, he agrees to go ahead and kill Duncan.

Build critical skills

Read Macbeth's soliloquy carefully and identify the lines which list his reservations:
- Fear of punishment.
- Duncan is his king, his relative and his guest.
- Duncan is a good man.

GRADE **BOOSTER**

The imagery in Macbeth and Lady Macbeth's speeches indicates great contrasts in their characters. His language is unsure, indicating a troubled conscience. Hers is manipulative and violent. 'Screw your courage to the sticking place' refers to the way the tension of violin strings is adjusted to play the right note. This is exactly how she is 'playing' her husband in the scene. Explanation of the effects of complex imagery will raise your grade.

Act 2 scene 1

An atmosphere of evil and tension is evident as Banquo and Fleance comment on the dark night. Banquo jokes about money-saving actions in heaven – blowing out the candles (because there is no moonlight and no stars). This reminds the audience of Lady Macbeth's wish for the smoke of hell to cover their deeds.

Banquo says he is unable to sleep – the witches have corrupted him, too – but he only gives in to 'cursed thoughts' in his dreams, contrasting with the action Macbeth is about to take.

Macbeth enters and both men are surprised to find the other awake. Banquo hands Macbeth a diamond for his 'kind hostess', who, ironically, has just ensured Duncan's death. Macbeth replies that they would have done more, if they had had longer notice. His awkward expression betrays tension and guilt.

They speak about their encounter with the weird sisters: Banquo admits to dreaming about them. Macbeth lies that he 'think[s] not of them' and suggests that he will honour Banquo if the prediction about becoming king should come true. The irony – he is about to ensure exactly that – will not be lost on the audience.

Banquo leaves Macbeth alone on stage.

Macbeth's second soliloquy begins with one of Shakespeare's most famous lines. There are different ways of interpreting this 'dagger'. Are we to think that Macbeth's mind plays tricks as he obsesses about what he is about to do, conjuring up a hallucination of a dagger pointing towards the room of the sleeping king? Or, have the witches intervened, coaxing him to do the deed by sending a real dagger?

Build critical skills

Note how directors present the dagger on stage and screen: some have a dagger, suggesting that there is something there, and some do not, implying that it is an illusion. How do you interpret this speech?

Build critical skills

This scene introduces us to Banquo's son, Fleance. Macbeth has no children. How might the witches' promise that Banquo's descendants will become king cause a rift in the men's friendship?

Key quotation

...*a false creation,*
Proceeding from the
heat-oppressed brain.
(2.1 38–39)

Build critical skills

If you were directing this scene, would you show the murder, or keep it off-stage? Why? What effect would you create?

Build critical skills

As a soldier, Macbeth must be used to the sight of blood: remind yourself of the gory descriptions of his exploits on the battlefield in Act 1 scene 2. Why does the sight of Duncan's blood provoke such an extreme reaction? What happened in the bedchamber to cause him to feel intense guilt?

Macbeth takes his eyes off the dagger, convincing himself there is nothing there, then looks again to see it covered in 'gouts of blood'. What does this indicate to you about his state of mind?

Is he talking himself into a murdering frame of mind by thinking evil thoughts? He describes himself as 'Murder' personified as he begins to walk towards the bedroom, begging the stones beneath his feet to keep his footsteps quiet.

The bell rings and he takes it as a signal that all is ready for Duncan's death.

The **rhyming couplet** at the end of the scene, with its reference to a funeral knell, signifies the end of more than the speech: it is the end of King Duncan's life.

Act 2 scene 2

The contrasting characters of Macbeth and Lady Macbeth are revealed by their reactions to the murder of Duncan.

Lady Macbeth has been drinking: she claims it has made her braver, however, her jumpy state contradicts her words. She says Duncan's resemblance to her father prevented her from performing the murder. From a woman who claims she could have battered her own baby's brains out, this might make us question how much of her callousness is real and how much is bravado put on for her husband.

When Macbeth returns, their conversation shows how tense they both are. Each of them jumps at the slightest noise. Macbeth worries that they may have woken others: their biggest fear is being found out but Macbeth's conscience torments him when he looks at the blood on his hands.

Lady Macbeth reassures him that simply washing his hands will solve the problem – then notices he is still carrying the daggers. He refuses to go back and she mocks him saying she will return them and smear even more blood on the grooms. (Notice the pun on gilt/guilt, repeated by Macbeth in the next scene.)

She goes into the bedchamber while Macbeth, deaf to knocking at the castle gates, stares at his 'hangman's hands'. He imagines all the water in the ocean failing to wash away his sin.

Returning, Lady Macbeth prods him into action. They must appear to have been in bed when the gate is opened. Her words contrast with his.

Key quotation

A little water clears us of this deed...

(2.2 70)

▲ Macbeth after murdering Duncan.

There is irony in this statement: water may wash blood off the hands, but it takes more than that to cleanse the soul, as will become apparent later.

Act 2 scene 3

The knocking at the castle gate links the two scenes together. The tension as the audience wonders whether Macbeth will be found out is now broken by a scene of **comic relief**.

GRADE *BOOSTER*

This element of the play's structure gives the audience a break, a chance to relax and to laugh at the porter's words and antics. However, there is a dark side to the porter's words. Showing that you appreciate the relevance of this scene will gain you marks.

The porter's opening words, though comic, link with the evil-doing of the previous scenes, as he imagines himself to be the porter at the gates of hell, an example of **dramatic irony**. He mentions Beelzebub, a devil, and imagines he is admitting sinners.

He opens the gate, explaining to Macduff and Lennox that the servants were drinking until three in the morning. He jokes about the effects of too much alcohol – a red nose, sleep and urination, also '**equivocation**' as regards sex: drink makes a man want it, but takes away his capability.

Macduff responds light-heartedly. However, tension returns as Macbeth appears and Macduff asks if the king is awake and goes to the bedchamber. Lennox describes strange events overnight: strong winds, screams, earthquakes, all of which reflect the unnatural murder of the king.

Macbeth's tension shows in his terse reply. Like the audience, his focus is on Macduff's discovery. Chaos erupts as he returns, reflecting the destruction of sanctity and order that the king represented. Macduff orders the bell to be rung to wake everyone and the stage fills with noise and running people.

Lady Macbeth's acting skills are evident as she responds to the 'news'. Note the irony of Macduff's comment that he cannot speak the words to her:

The repetition, in a woman's ear,

Would murder as it fell.

(2.3 78–79)

Both she and Macbeth react in a suspicious way: Banquo notes her comment that the death was 'In our house'. Macbeth returns with Lennox, whose description of the murder scene is the nearest we get to seeing the dead king, while Macbeth's expression of grief is increasingly

---

Build critical skills

The three sinners that the porter describes are a farmer who has committed suicide, an equivocator and a tailor who has stolen cloth from the garments he is making. Can you connect these sins with other events, characters or themes in the play?

Equivocation: a manner of speaking when a person uses words in an ambiguous or untrustworthy way – to mislead (see *Themes* p. 56).

Key quotation

...where we are

There's daggers in men's smiles: the near in blood

The nea'er bloody.

(2.3 132–134)

extravagant in its imagery: 'the fountain of your blood/Is stopped', 'His silver skin laced with his golden blood' (reflecting the 'gilt' of the blood on the servants). Macbeth claims he killed the servants in fury. Lady Macbeth's faint interrupts his outpourings but raises the suspicions of anyone watching closely, particularly Banquo. Macbeth regains control and sends everyone to dress.

The king's sons, Malcolm and Donalbain, decide to separate for safety – Malcolm to England and Donalbain to Ireland. Unlike their trusting father, they understand that appearances can be deceptive.

Act 2 scene 4

Ross and the Old Man explore the strange events after Duncan's death. Though it is daytime, it is still dark – a reference to the belief that the sun never rose on the day of Christ's crucifixion, emphasising the link between God and the king.

Unnatural happenings among animals reflect the chaos in the human world: an owl is said to have killed a falcon and the horses in Duncan's stable have gone wild and eaten each other. This reminds us that the witches' supernatural powers can turn the natural world upside down, and that Macbeth is under their evil spell.

Macduff brings news, appearing to agree that the likely murderers are the dead servants, though says the king's sons are also suspects since they ran away. He says Macbeth has been named as king, in Malcolm's absence, and has gone to Scone to be crowned, while Duncan's body has been buried at Colme-Hill, the tomb of Scottish kings.

Macduff indicates distrust of Macbeth, saying he will not attend the coronation. His words reflect recurring imagery of clothing, expressing fears that: 'Our old robes sit easier than our new', implying that the rule of Duncan will turn out to be better than that of the new king, Macbeth.

Act 3 scene 1

Banquo opens the scene with a soliloquy, sharing thoughts he dare not speak to anyone else.

He wonders whether the promise made to him will also come true. This is ironic, as the original audience of the play would be aware that King James descended from Banquo's line.

Banquo is joined by Macbeth, whose ability to manipulate and deceive is shown when he insists on Banquo's attendance at the Macbeths' feast that night. Note the parallels with Macbeth and Lady Macbeth's roles as hosts when they planned the death of Duncan (see Grade booster p. 18).

Build critical skills

Banquo recalls the promises the weird sisters made. He says that Macbeth now 'has it all', though he has his suspicions about what Macbeth has done to become king. What is the evidence of his doubts?

Macbeth seizes at the cover story that the king's sons are suspected of 'cruel parricide', grabbing every opportunity to shift suspicion from himself.

Banquo leaves and Macbeth dismisses his courtiers, then asks for some anonymous men to be brought to him.

GRADE BOOSTER

Macbeth and Lady Macbeth seem to swap roles as the play progresses: he hardens while she becomes more vulnerable. The exact placement of their soliloquies in the play reveals this to the audience. Commenting effectively on links and parallels of this sort will raise your marks.

Macbeth speaks his third soliloquy (3.1 47–71), justifying his plans. There is no agonising in this speech, unlike in the previous soliloquies.

He asks for the aid of fate, as he did when he said that 'chance' might bring him Duncan's crown. However, later events show that fate is not what he has in mind.

Two men are now persuaded that Banquo is their enemy, the person who held them back. Macbeth adopts Lady Macbeth's tactic, suggesting that if they are real men, they will take revenge.

Macbeth explains that his part in the deed must be hidden from those who still support Banquo, then reaffirms that Fleance's death is as important to him as his father's.

Build critical skills

Note that Lady Macbeth is absent from the plans for this double murder. Macbeth is now working independently of her. How will this affect her?

He ends with a rhyming couplet, similar to the one he spoke just before he killed Duncan. It underlines the finality of his plan.

Banquo, thy soul's flight

If it find heaven, must find it out tonight.

(3.1 140–141)

GRADE BOOSTER

Remember that rhyming couplets are used structurally to end scenes in order to clarify where the action of the play is going, increase tension or underline one of the themes.

Build critical skills

Macbeth wants Banquo out of the way. Identify the three questions he asks, in among all the polite chat, checking exactly where Banquo will be.

Build critical skills

Look carefully at Macbeth's third soliloquy. Which lines reveal Macbeth's three reasons for his decision that Banquo must die?

Find a line that shows Macbeth now seems concerned about punishment in the afterlife – contradicting his earlier soliloquy in Act 1 scene 7.

Act 3 scene 2

Lady Macbeth asks the servant if Banquo has left. She seems suspicious and troubled, her words reflecting Macbeth's insecurity: 'where our desire is got without content.' However, her tone changes when Macbeth enters. She soothes him, suggesting he stops worrying about 'things without all remedy'.

Macbeth pours out his fear and regret. He says they have only achieved part of their goal ('scorched [injured] the snake, not killed it'). He talks of the 'terrible dreams' that interrupt their sleep and is envious of Duncan's peace in death, where trouble cannot touch him.

Lady Macbeth reminds him to appear cheerful for their guests and he agrees that they must carry on the pretence that all is well. He hints at dark deeds, mentioning Banquo and Fleance, warning that before night ends 'there shall be done/A deed of dreadful note.' He refuses to confide in her, closing the scene by asking 'seeling night' to hide the world, reminding us of Lady Macbeth's appeal for darkness in Act 1 scene 5.

Act 3 scene 3

This scene is short but brutal. A mysterious stranger joins the murderers, saying Macbeth has sent him. Night falls and he hears horses. He seems to know the way Banquo usually approaches the castle on foot.

The light Fleance carries is put out and the three killers set upon Banquo.

As Banquo is dying, he shouts out to save his son's life, giving him a final command to take revenge for this terrible act.

Act 3 scene 4

GRADE BOOSTER

> If any one scene in Macbeth shows the change from order to chaos in Macbeth's Scotland, this is it. Demonstrating your understanding of how the structure of scenes helps to advance themes will raise your grade.

The stately ritual of a court banquet, with Macbeth and his queen in their full royal robes, opens the scene. Macbeth requests his guests to seat themselves according to their rank, saying: 'You know your own degrees', though ironically he is occupying a place he has no right to.

Macbeth soon abandons the behaviour expected of a host, leaving his wife in charge of entertaining his guests. He goes to a dark corner to speak to the murderer, reminding us how he left the room when he was entertaining Duncan.

Build critical skills

Investigate how parallels and links between speeches (like this one between Macbeth's appeal to night and Lady Macbeth's appeal for darkness) help to remind the audience of important themes in the play.

Build critical skills

It is sometimes suggested that Macbeth is the third killer, come to ensure that the job is done properly. What is your opinion about this?

Why does Shakespeare show us the death of Banquo on stage, in contrast to the murder of Duncan off stage?

The conversation is tense and furtive: he is delighted that Banquo is dead, but agitated to hear that Fleance escaped. He repeats the earlier image comparing Banquo with an injured snake, saying that though the 'grown serpent' is dead, 'the worm', currently harmless, will become poisonous eventually.

Lady Macbeth reminds Macbeth of his duties. He returns to the table, expressing regret that Banquo has not arrived. Lennox and Ross invite him to take a seat, and, during this exchange, the ghost of Banquo appears, so Macbeth can see no empty place.

Macbeth's guests notice his state – however, Lady Macbeth takes control, reassuring them that this is normal behaviour. Taking Macbeth to one side, she questions his manhood and accuses him of being a coward, techniques which succeeded earlier. Macbeth only regains control when the ghost disappears, and his wife reminds him he has guests. While raising a toast to Banquo, he sees the ghost again.

Lady Macbeth accuses her husband of disrupting the banquet with 'admired disorder' and dismisses the bewildered guests. The banquet ends in a chaotic manner as she tells her guests to 'stand not on the order of your going', dispensing with the usual rules of hierarchy. This is ironic, as Macbeth upset the natural order the moment the sinful thought of killing the king crossed his mind.

After their guests have left, Macbeth's words are dark and guilty. He fears the consequences of murder: 'blood will have blood' and asks why Macduff was not at the banquet. He ends the scene stating his intention to visit the weird sisters for more information, saying he is too far in to turn back.

Act 3 scene 5

This scene appears in most copies of the play, though is often omitted in production. It shows Hecate, Queen of the witches, scolding the witches for playing games with Macbeth without consulting her. She makes ominous sounding plans for his visit to them the next day.

Act 3 scene 6

Here Shakespeare summarises information quickly to move the action on to the interesting event of Macbeth visiting the witches. Lennox summarises events in Scotland, in a guarded, ironic way that shows he knows that Macbeth is responsible for all the murders.

Another Lord says Malcolm is in England at the court of Edward the Confessor, where Macduff has joined them, hoping to raise an army against Macbeth. This followed his refusal to meet Macbeth after the banquet.

> **Build critical skills**
>
> Some stage productions do not show the ghost, just Macbeth talking madly to thin air. Some film versions adopt special effects, such as making the ghost transparent. How would you choose to present the ghost?

> **Key quotation**
>
> *Take any shape but* that, *and my firm nerves*
> *Shall never tremble.*
> (3.4 102–103)

▲ Macbeth in royal robes.

Build critical skills

How does each vision in Act 4 scene 1 link with the prophecy that accompanies it? And how does each prophecy support or contradict any other?

Build critical skills

The pattern of three promises about Macbeth's future with one about Banquo's exactly parallels Act 1 scene 3. How does this remind you of the influence the witches have in instigating events so far?

GRADE BOOSTER

Messengers are often used like narrators to avoid having to slow down the action with extra scenes. Examples include Macbeth's servant speaking to Macduff, Macduff's arrival in England and the nobles of Scotland losing trust in their king. Understanding that certain scenes have a summarising function will demonstrate a sophisticated understanding of the play's structure.

Act 4 scene 1

The scene mirrors the opening of the play: the witches prepare for Macbeth's arrival by reciting a rhyming spell and cooking up an evil potion in a cauldron.

A desperate Macbeth bursts into the scene and demands answers to his questions. The witches offer him the option of hearing from their 'masters' (evil spirits) and he chooses this.

- Apparition 1, described as 'an armed head', warns Macbeth to 'Beware the Thane of Fife' (Macduff).
- Apparition 2, described as a 'a bloody child', promises 'none of woman born/Shall harm Macbeth.'
- Apparition 3, a child prince carrying a tree, described by Macbeth as: 'like the issue of a king/And wears...the round and top of sovereignty', promises that 'Macbeth shall never vanquished be until/Great Birnam wood to high Dunsinane hill/Shall come against him.'
- Apparition 4 shows Macbeth a vision. Macbeth, not content with good news, asks about Banquo's line coming to rule. He describes what he sees as 'too like the spirit of Banquo', wearing 'a crown [that] does sear mine eyeballs' – and similar figures 'stretch[ed] out t' the crack of doom'. The last in line 'bears a glass/Which shows me many more.' Finally, 'the blood-boltered Banquo' appears and 'points at them for his'.

The witches disappear as Lennox arrives. He brings news that the audience already knows: Macduff is in England. Macbeth's reaction is swift and ruthless. He has been promised he has no one to fear, yet, unable to harm Macduff, he decides to send killers to Macduff's castle to slaughter his entire family.

GRADE BOOSTER

The first time Macbeth meets the witches their morality can be seen as ambiguous. They simply foretell the future. This time, both they and he are linked with the powers of darkness. He is under their spell as he plans to murder innocent women and children. Commenting on this significant development will gain you marks.

Act 4 scene 2

This scene, where Macbeth sends murderers to kill Macduff's family, is discussed in detail in *Language, style and analysis* on pp. 60–62.

Act 4 scene 3

This is a complicated scene, exploring ideas of what a good king might be and reinforcing the belief that the king is chosen by God.

> **GRADE** *BOOSTER*
>
> The only scene in the play that takes place in England, this emphasises the union of the English and Scottish powers against the evil of Macbeth. In this way, it celebrates King James' accession to the throne of both countries and reinforces his rightful position as ruler. Demonstrating your understanding of contextual significance of this kind could raise your grade.

Macduff and Malcolm lament Macbeth's damage to Scotland. The events of the preceding scene are juxtaposed with this in a way that leads to dramatic irony: although Macduff has no idea that Macbeth has murdered his family, he talks about men and women being murdered:

> …Each new morn
>
> New widows howl, new orphans cry…

(4.3 4–5)

Malcolm suggests that Macduff may be in allegiance with Macbeth and may intend to betray him, saying (ironically):

> He hath not touched you yet.

(4.3 14)

He expresses doubt about Macduff leaving his family unprotected in Scotland if he genuinely sees Macbeth as an enemy. This raises audience anticipation of how Macduff will react when he hears the news about the murder of his family.

Shakespeare uses Malcolm to help the audience consider what makes a good king.

Build critical skills

Look at this list of 'King-becoming graces':

…justice, verity, temperance, stableness,

Bounty, perseverance, mercy, lowliness,

Devotion, patience, courage, fortitude…

(4.3 92–94)

Consider how many of these qualities King Duncan had, compared with Macbeth.

GRADE *BOOSTER*

Macbeth's tyrannical rule, and the atrocities he has committed in Scotland, are contrasted with the goodness of Malcolm and King Edward. The audience is reminded of the very different way Duncan ruled Scotland. This is important to your understanding of the structure of the play as a tragedy.

Malcolm concludes with lines supposedly describing himself, but which summarise what Macbeth's rule has achieved in Scotland:

...had I power, I should

Pour the milk of concord into hell,

Uproot the universal peace,

Confound all unity on earth.

(4.3 97–100)

Macduff, devastated, pours out his grief at the end of hope for his country. Malcolm's test has worked: he is sure Macduff supports him and he states how truly virtuous he is. Better still, he already has an army of 10,000 men ready to invade Scotland to reclaim his crown.

A third good king is held up for comparison with Macbeth: the saintly Edward the Confessor, who had the power to cure the disease scrofula with his touch. His descendants, including James I, were said to share this power. This is a direct comparison with the deathly rule of Macbeth.

Ross arrives from Scotland with terrible news for Macduff. The audience already knows it, so there is enormous tension as Ross plays for time before revealing what has happened.

Ross hints that dreadful deeds continue, reflecting Macduff's opening description of Macbeth's atrocities: 'groans and shrieks that rend the air' reminds us that Lady Macduff left the stage screaming as she tried to run from the murderers.

Malcolm and Macduff question Ross who replies evasively, speaking of the need for Malcolm to lead troops to Scotland to incite Scots to fight against Macbeth. Finally, he hints that he has some terrible news and that it is for Macduff. He still cannot bring himself to say the words until Macduff suggests that he can guess, then it tumbles out:

Your castle is surprised; your wife and babes

Savagely slaughtered...

(4.3 205–206)

Macduff reacts passionately. He seems unable take in these words, asking if 'all' his family were killed. He reminds the audience of the comparison of the children with birds in a nest when he calls Macbeth a 'hell-kite'.

He reminds us that Macbeth has no children, implying that a father could not have carried out such an atrocity. We are also reminded of the proper behaviour of a man when Macduff answers Malcolm's advice to 'Dispute it like a man', saying that he must first feel the sadness and pain of his loss to be a proper man.

By the end of the scene, Macduff resolves to fight alongside Malcolm for the freedom of his country, but now has a personal reason for wanting revenge on Macbeth.

Macbeth now truly should 'Beware Macduff.'

Act 5 scene 1

Back in Scotland, we hear that great changes have taken place in Lady Macbeth since the last time she was on stage, after the banquet. A gentlewoman says Lady Macbeth has been sleepwalking, reading and writing on paper she keeps in a locked cupboard. The gentlewoman tells the doctor she 'will not' repeat the words Lady Macbeth has spoken.

Lady Macbeth appears on stage in her nightgown, carrying a light, which her gentlewoman says is always by her.

Her conscience is troubling her: she constantly rubs her hands, as if trying to wash them. She recalls all the deaths she and her husband have been responsible for.

> **Build critical skills**
>
> Read the speech (from lines 31–61) and identify which lines refer to the deaths – in this order:
> - Duncan (where she *did* get blood on her hands)
> - Banquo
> - Duncan again
> - the Macduff family
> - Banquo again
> - Duncan again
> - Banquo again
> - and finally back to Duncan

Note the irony of Lady Macbeth's words and actions: she told Macbeth that 'a little water clears us of this deed' after Duncan's murder, yet now she cannot get the blood, even the smell of it, off her hands. She advised sleep as a cure, yet now she is unable to sleep soundly.

Shakespeare seems to imply that her plea to the evil spirits to make her immune to guilt was futile. She is a woman, with a woman's feelings and conscience. The witches said they could torture humans by preventing them from sleeping (Act 1 scene 3) and Macbeth himself feared that he had 'murdered sleep' (Act 2 scene 2) when he killed the sleeping Duncan. Lady Macbeth is presented as the casualty of their actions.

> **Build critical skills**
>
> The lack of female characters in *Macbeth* is particularly striking. This gentlewoman in Act 5 scene 1 is the only other female character we have seen at the castle. The guests at the banquet were all male. What impact would this have had on Lady Macbeth after the close bond with her husband is broken?

> **Build critical skills**
>
> There are many contrasts in this scene with the woman who wished for darkness to cover the evil deeds she was planning. How do her expressions of guilt remind you of her husband's before and after he killed Duncan?

GRADE BOOSTER

Many short scenes are now juxtaposed to show what happens as each side prepares for battle. This creates pace and tension for the audience. Showing understanding of such structure devices will help boost your marks.

Key quotation

Now does he feel his title

Hang loose about him,
like a giant's robe

Upon a dwarfish thief.
(5.2 20–22)

GRADE BOOSTER

Note that Act 5 scene 1 is almost entirely written in prose – the form usually used for lower status characters. Lady Macbeth previously spoke in powerful blank verse but now her language is breaking down as her mind disintegrates. Commenting on features of dramatic style like this will help you reach the higher grades.

Act 5 scene 2

The Thanes show us that Macbeth is losing his hold over Scotland. Lady Macbeth is not the only one who is behaving in an insane manner. Imagery connected with clothing, which has shadowed Macbeth's role as king since the start of the play, is picked up again here.

Those who have deserted Macbeth march towards Malcolm, the rightful heir. The witches' words are brought to mind by the mention of Birnam Wood.

Act 5 scene 3

Macbeth's behaviour is wild: his mood swings from fearless bravado, to unwarranted fury at his servant's fear, to brief regret as he reflects on the old age he would have liked:

…honour, love, obedience, troops of friends

I must not look to have…

(5.3 25–26)

He faces the fight with purpose, putting on his armour as he talks to the doctor, placing Lady Macbeth's health in his hands. The distance between the couple is extreme. We never see them together on stage again. He appeals almost light-heartedly to the doctor to find a cure for Scotland, asking for laxatives like rhubarb and senna to 'purge' away the English army.

Macbeth speaks about Birnam Wood at the start and end of the scene, showing how desperately he clings to the witches' promises. He is doomed by his misplaced trust.

Act 5 scene 4

When Malcolm tells each soldier to camouflage himself with a tree branch, the audience begins to understand that the witches' promises have all been tricks, as Banquo warned Macbeth.

Act 5 scene 5

In Macbeth's castle, we see the re-emergence of the brave soldier he was at the start of the play. He prepares for a siege, still clinging for security to the witches' promises, sure that his castle can withstand the enemy army. This creates anticipation in the audience, waiting for his reaction when he sees the moving 'trees'.

The sound of crying women distracts him.

Shakespeare shows how Macbeth has changed since he murdered Duncan in this brief final soliloquy:

> The time has been, my senses would have cooled
>
> To hear a night-shriek…
>
> (5.5 10–11)

His murderous acts have dulled his reactions: 'I have supped full with horrors', he says (5.5 13).

His servant, Seyton, brings him news that Lady Macbeth has died.

At the end of the play it is suggested that she has committed suicide.

Macbeth's speech on hearing the news of Lady Macbeth's death is an **aside**, spoken in the presence of a servant, though not for his ears. Macbeth previously reflected on his feelings of loss when he saw his troops deserting to fight with the English army. He stands alone as all he hoped to gain from his evil deeds slips away.

The first line perhaps means that it would have been more convenient if his wife had died when he had time to grieve, after the battle. Perhaps he is being fatalistic, saying she would have died eventually, so what difference does it make?

He again talks about how senseless life is. He talks about the 'petty pace' of time passing, imagining the days ahead creeping on pointlessly until he dies.

Three metaphors for life reflect Macbeth's feelings of disillusionment: 'Brief candle', 'a poor player/that struts and frets his hour upon the stage/and then is heard no more' and 'A tale told by an idiot… signifying nothing.'

Macbeth's despondency is interrupted by the news that Birnam Wood is moving. A messenger says he has seen with his own eyes: 'a moving grove'. Macbeth is confused and shows, first, disbelief about the news and anger towards the bearer. He then begins to wonder whether the witches have tricked him, speaking an aside which echoes Banquo's earlier warning.

Build critical skills

Do you remember the reservations about Malcolm's prowess as a soldier that were raised in Act 1? Kings conventionally led troops into battle. Like his father, Duncan, Malcolm 'leads from behind'. How might an audience react to this?

The scene ends with a reminder of the brave soldier Macbeth was at the start of the play:

> Ring the alarum bell! Blow wind! Come wrack!

> At least we'll die with harness on our back.

> (5.5 50–51)

The rhyming couplet contrasts with the despairing tone of the middle of the scene, changing to one of decisiveness and resolution as Macbeth heads out to fight the English army.

Act 5 scene 6

This is the shortest scene in the play as the action heats up: outside Macbeth's castle, Malcolm tells his troops to throw down their branches. He gives Old Siward and his son instructions to lead his men into battle. He and Macduff will follow.

Macduff orders the battle trumpets to be sounded – a sound heard throughout the battle that follows.

Act 5 scene 7

This is another short, pacy scene: Macbeth defends his castle gates, hanging on grimly to the promise that 'none of woman born' can harm him. He meets Young Siward, they fight and Macbeth kills him. Macbeth exits, reassured, gloating that he is invulnerable.

As he leaves, Macduff appears, sword ready for action. Malcolm and Old Siward now find the castle's defences have been overcome. Macbeth's army is split in two, fighting for each side. Malcolm has little to do to win the battle as his men enter the castle.

Act 5 scene 8

Macbeth, alone, briefly speaks about suicide in the Roman manner of falling on one's sword to escape dishonourable capture. He decides to fight on, as Macduff enters. Macbeth expresses some feelings of guilt about the suffering he has already caused to Macduff:

> my soul is too much charged

> With blood of thine already.

> (5.8 5–6)

and warns him

I bear a charmed life, which must not yield

To one of woman born.

(5.8 12–13)

Macduff's reply is the end of all hope for Macbeth.

Macbeth's shock reflects that of the audience as they realise the promises which seemed so secure *were* all true, but not in the way they seemed to be. The equivocation of the witches is summed up as Macbeth realises how thoroughly they have tricked him:

…be these juggling fiends no more believed

That palter with us in a double sense.

(5.8 19–20)

Macbeth refuses to fight until Macduff calls him a coward and orders him to surrender. Though it is obvious now that Macbeth has no hope of surviving, he holds his shield in front of him and goes in to fight his nemesis. This fight is action packed and goes on for some time: it is no easy victory for Macduff and an exciting experience for the audience.

It ends with Macbeth's death and Macduff's triumph.

> **Build critical skills**
>
> Note that Shakespeare did not write the stage directions which end the scene. Do you think Macbeth should die on stage? Or do you think the final sight of Macbeth alive should be as he exits the stage fighting, reminding us of the first description we had of him?

Act 5 scene 9

Malcolm and Old Siward check who is missing, naming Young Siward and Macduff. Ross brings news that Siward's son has been killed in action.

They are interrupted by the missing Macduff, carrying something which would profoundly affect the audience: Macbeth's head. This was the customary punishment for traitors: a reminder of the execution of the original Thane of Cawdor.

Macduff is the first to greet Malcolm with his new title, King of Scotland.

> **GRADE BOOSTER**
>
> Malcolm's final speech restores order to the country, replacing the chaos of Macbeth's reign. This speech nods to how King James unified Scotland and England. The inclusion of well-integrated contextual references like this can enhance your work and boost your grade.

Key quotation

This dead butcher and his fiend-like queen.

(5.9 36)

Like his father, Malcolm rewards those who have fought bravely with the English title of 'Earl', rather than the Scottish 'Thane'. He repeats Duncan's metaphor of planting and growth. He promises to call home those who have left the country for fear of Macbeth, reminding us of his brother, Donalbain. He pronounces the epitaph of Macbeth and Lacy Macbeth, hinting that her death was suicide.

The play ends with the promise of a new start for Scotland as Malcolm invites those who have fought with him to attend his coronation at Scone.

Structure

The overarching structure of *Macbeth* owes something to classical Greek tragedy, in that fate causes the downfall of a great man. The play's structure likewise describes a descent like the downward rotation of a wheel from top (zenith) to bottom (nadir).

In Greek tragedy the action begins with order and the success of a noble man. Downward motion may be brought about from **fate** (for example, the witches influence on events) or may result from a **flaw of character** in the hero. In Macbeth's case, this is ambition (see *Themes* pp. 51–53), which leads him to commit all the acts that cause chaos in Scotland – and his death – at the bottom of the wheel.

At the end of the drama, a new force for good restores order, and thus the inevitable rotation of the wheel will begin again.

Key quotation

Ross to Lady Macduff:

Things at their worst will cease, or else climb upward

To what they were before.

(4.2 24–25)

GRADE *FOCUS*

Your exam task will never ask you to write a plot summary of the play, however there are marks given for AO1 for your response to the text, and for your ability to select evidence, whether quoted or by reference. AO2 rewards comments on the structure of a text.

Grade 5

Students will be able to show a clear and detailed understanding of explicit and implicit meanings of the whole text and of the effects created by its structure. They will be able to select and comment on relevant references from the text.

Grade 8

Students' responses will display a comprehensive critical understanding of explicit and implicit meanings in the text as a whole and will examine and evaluate the writer's use of structure in detail. They will be able to select precise references and show insight in their comments.

REVIEW YOUR LEARNING

1 List all the deaths which occur in the play – in order.

2 Who discovers Duncan's dead body?

3 Why is the Porter's scene (start of Act 2 scene 3) included in the play?

4 What does Lady Macbeth do at the end of the banquet (Act 3 scene 4)?

5 Why does Macbeth send murderers to kill Macduff's family?

6 How does Birnam Wood come to Dunsinane?

7 How does the ending of the play reflect the opening?

8 Who has the bigger impact on the way the plot develops: the witches or Lady Macbeth?

Answers on pp. 109–110.

Characterisation

Target your thinking

- How does Shakespeare present his characters? (**AO2**)
- What functions do characters serve in the play? (**AO1** and **AO3**)

Build critical skills

Remind yourself of the meaning of the word 'equivocation' (see p. 21).

The main characters in *Macbeth* are ambiguous and not always what they appear to be at face value. Which major theme of the play does this connect them with? How does appearance differ from reality?

It is important to note that when writing about *Macbeth* it is impossible to separate the author's use of characterisation from the themes of the play. The examples given below integrate both characters and themes throughout.

Methods of presenting characters on stage are straightforward:

- words – what a character says (in dialogue, or, particularly, in soliloquy)
- actions – what a character does
- words others say about the character
- events – and the character's involvement in them – and the effects of dramatic structure

The problem with *Macbeth* is that sometimes the words characters say are not the truth – sometimes they are downright lies, sometimes simply misleading. You will need to get under the surface of the evidence to interpret what the dialogue reveals.

Macbeth

Shakespeare introduces us to Macbeth in a manner which immediately makes him ambiguous. In the opening scene the witches plot to meet him, thus connecting him to evil at the very start of the play. Yet he is then presented to us by the Captain's description in Act 1 scene 2 as 'brave Macbeth', a fearless soldier, a man who fights on the side of right for his king, and who dispatches the king's enemies with ruthless efficiency.

GRADE *BOOSTER*

Remember that characters are constructs of the playwright, the director and the actor: you should not write about them as if they are real people.

Key quotation

...his brandished steel

Which smoked with bloody execution

...carved out his passage

Till he faced the slave...

Till he unseamed him from the nave to the chops...

(1.2 17–22)

An ambitious man

Macbeth's fatal flaw is his ambition, which is galvanised by the witches' prediction that he will become Thane of Cawdor and then king.

Build critical skills

Does Shakespeare offer clues that Macbeth already had unspoken desires to be king? He reacts to the witches' words by starting in surprise, then falling into spellbound silence. What might be going through his head?

When Macbeth receives the news that one of their promises has already come true, his thoughts immediately turn to murder, though he decides to leave fulfilment of the prediction to chance.

Key quotation

...Why do I yield to that suggestion,

Whose horrid image doth unfix my hair

And make my seated heart knock at my ribs...

(1.3 133–135)

Compare Macbeth's aside in Act 1 scene 3 lines 129–141 to his similarly dark words at the end of Act 1 scene 4. This speech combines the theme of fate (the witches, the timing of Duncan's announcements) with the strength of his sinful ambition to be the king.

Easily manipulated

Macbeth's response to the witches and Lady Macbeth's role in overcoming his crises of conscience suggest that he is, in the beginning, easily manipulated. Lady Macbeth recognises his ambition but also sees the obstacles to achieving what he wants. Her words imply that Macbeth is too good a man to go out and get something which is, at root, wrong. Yet she is sure she can change his mind. (See *Plot and structure* p. 17.)

Shakespeare clearly shows Macbeth being propelled towards evil by his wife. When he backtracks, listing reasons he should not commit the murder, she uses verbal and emotional arguments to persuade him, such as calling him a coward, questioning his manliness and reassuring him that their guilt can be concealed (Act 1 scene 7 lines 28–78). Despite his better judgement, he goes ahead with a murder which he knows is wrong.

However, although Macbeth may be manipulated by his wife in Acts 1 and 2, he goes on to murder Banquo without her input or knowledge. This manipulation is also an exploration of the nature of free will (see *Context* p. 9).

Build critical skills

The key quotation on p. 36 is a good example of how Shakespeare presents Macbeth as a puzzle for the audience. Is it good to be able to kill so brutally on the battlefield? What links the witches, apparently in league with the devil, with Macbeth?

Key quotation

...I fear thy nature...
is too full o' th' milk of
human kindness...

(1.5 14–15)

Key quotation

...thou wouldst be great
...but without the illness
should attend it...

That wouldst thou
holily...

(1.5 16–20)

A man with a conscience

Shakespeare presents Macbeth as a true tragic hero because of the combination of good and evil in his character. He does some appalling things, yet his conscience and imagination trouble and punish him. We see this through Shakespeare's use of soliloquies (see *Language, style and analysis* pp. 62–63). Any essay about Macbeth's character will require close attention to how Shakespeare presents his changing character through these speeches.

Macbeth's guilty conscience is revealed by means of subconscious imaginings and visions. His imagination is obvious from his first encounter with the witches (Act 1 scene 3), when he visualises murdering Duncan. However, the witches are not imaginary as Banquo also sees them and hears their words. Macbeth's guilty conscience before he kills Duncan is shown in his visions of accusing angels and cherubs (see *Language, style and analysis* p. 65), the dagger (see *Plot and structure* pp. 19–20), and the stones speaking out and giving him away.

Macbeth imagines night falling and the creatures of evil, 'night's black agents', gathering in the darkness as Banquo's murder is imminent. Afterwards he imagines ways the murder ('man of blood') might be revealed: moving stones, speaking trees, birds of ill omen. At the end of this scene, Shakespeare uses a powerful image of Macbeth crossing a river of blood.

> ...I am in blood
>
> Stepped in so far, that, should I wade no more,
>
> Returning were as tedious as go o'er.
>
> (3.4 136–138)

Banquo's ghost is more a matter for debate – is it a product of Macbeth's imagination? It could actually be there, though it is true that no one else sees anything sitting in Macbeth's own chair. Macbeth's second encounter with the witches and the apparitions they show him in Act 4 scene 1 could also be interpreted as imaginary.

Key quotation

Thou sure and firm-set earth,

Hear not my steps, which way they walk, for fear

Thy very stones prate of my whereabout...

(2.1 56–58)

Build critical skills

One interpretation of the play, sometimes explored in performance, is that the witches are ever present, for example, lending their powers to Lady Macbeth, dangling the dagger and setting the scene for Banquo's murder.

Either they seem to drive him almost mad, which means they must shoulder the blame for his actions, or his own deeds do, which means what happens is his fault. Which of these interpretations seems more valid to you, and why?

A tyrant

Once embarked on his descent into brutal violence, Macbeth's acts are shown by Shakespeare to be increasingly callous. He has spies everywhere. He lies to and cheats his one-time friend, Banquo, paying hired assassins to murder him and his son, Fleance, in a failed attempt to prevent Banquo's heirs becoming kings. Finally, taking heed of the witches' advice to 'be bloody, bold and resolute' (Act 4 scene 1), he commits the greatest atrocity in the play. Unable to reach Macduff, he orders all in Macduff's household to be massacred – a shocking act against the most vulnerable which would horrify audiences.

All of Scotland suffers under the rule of Macbeth, as shown in Malcolm's personification of the country.

Key quotation

Things bad begun make strong themselves by ill.

(3.2 55)

Key quotation

I think our country sinks beneath the yoke:

It weeps, it bleeds – and each new day a gash

Is added to her wounds.

(4.3 39–41)

Macduff's words in Act 4 scene 3 offer an ironic description of the state of the country as, unknown to him, his family are Macbeth's latest victims. This is an important image of Macbeth as a despotic leader who is destroying Scotland and its people. Many lines in this scene emphasise how Macbeth's power is maintained by fear.

At the end of the play, Macbeth is described as a 'dead butcher' – quite a fall from the god-like war hero who fought the Norwegians single-handed at the start.

Brave soldier to the end

At the end of the play Macbeth is alone and half crazy, clinging on to the security of the witches' promises. His wife is mad with guilt, but he is so detached from her he can feel nothing. As the English army approaches, his troops desert to fight on the opposite side: we might well see him as reaping what he has sown. However, there is a moment when Shakespeare's words remind us of Macbeth's awareness of how pointless all his actions have been. His wife dies, he realises he has been tricked by the witches when he sees the trees of Birnam Wood moving, and for a moment it is almost possible for the audience to feel sorry for him. (See *Plot and structure* p. 31.)

Macbeth ends the play as he started, a soldier and a man of action on the battlefield. He even fights on with Macduff, knowing that his death is certain, rather than be called a coward or taken prisoner, so there are elements of the hero still present at his death. However, the final scene remembers him as a usurper, cursed, a tyrant and a butcher.

Lady Macbeth

Shakespeare presents the heroine as a stronger character than her husband for much of the first half of the play, a reversal of the typical gender roles of the time. However, by the end, any initial judgement that she is a kind of tragic heroine in her own right has long been dismissed.

A fourth weird sister?

Lady Macbeth is introduced as she reads the letter Macbeth has sent, describing his meeting with the witches. She is presented as both decisive and brutal in her reasoning that, in order for Macbeth to become king, he must murder Duncan.

Key quotation

Hie thee hither

That I may...chastise with the valour of my tongue

All that impedes thee from the golden round.

(1.5 23–26)

Unlike Macbeth, she does not reflect on reservations of conscience. Whereas Macbeth was chosen by the weird sisters and tempted by their promise, she invites them into her body – and indeed her soul – as she summons the evil spirits to 'unsex her' and to take away her ability to nurture children: in other words, to make her into a man capable of doing such evil.

Look closely at Lady Macbeth's soliloquy in Act 1 scene 5 (lines 36–52). The speech is central to your understanding of her character. It is discussed on p. 17. There is also an extract-based essay answer on pp. 84–92.

Her closeness to her husband is unquestionable. Bear in mind that there are few female characters in the play and Lady Macbeth's only relationship is shown to be that with her husband. Directors interpret the physical relationship between the couple differently.

Her deviousness and powers of manipulation are obvious: when Duncan arrives, she conceals her thoughts and acts the perfect hostess as she welcomes him into her home for his final night on earth. She entertains him while her husband leaves the room to grapple with his conscience.

Build critical skills

Remember that all female roles, including Lady Macbeth, would have been played by boy actors in Shakespeare's time. What implications of this can you see for the scenes with Macbeth and his wife?

Build critical skills

On the surface, Lady Macbeth – with her strength of character and her murderous intentions – is far from a stereotypical woman, and yet what impressions of her do you form from her soliloquy in Act 1 scene 5?

Is she basically a loyal and supportive wife? Is she really evil if she needs to call for the help of the devil to kill? Is she ambitious for herself?

Practical and cold

Lady Macbeth's contribution to Duncan's murder goes beyond ensuring her husband's will to do it. She makes all the practical arrangements, lays out the daggers and drugs the king's guards. Perhaps here, when she is alone as Macbeth goes to do the deed, Shakespeare hints at a chink in her armour: her words reveal that she has been drinking to overcome her fear, and also show that she has some 'feminine' feelings of affection.

Key quotation

Had he not resembled
My father as he slept, I had done't.
(2.2 12–13)

Once Macbeth is back, quite clearly beside himself with guilt, her strength returns. There is a symbiotic element to their relationship: she is presented as stronger when he needs her – when he is most weak. As the play unfolds, we see them drift away from each other: his career of tyranny continues without her support and she falls apart.

Shakespeare contrasts Lady Macbeth's earlier confident statement that

A little water clears us of this deed.

(2.2 70)

with her demented handwashing in the sleepwalking scene to demonstrate the extent of her disintegration.

▲ In some productions Lady Macbeth uses her charms to seduce her husband into committing the murder that, on his own, he would never have done.

Build critical skills

When Macbeth's bizarre eulogy to Duncan looks as if it could cause suspicion, Lady Macbeth fakes a faint to draw attention away from him – or does she? Is this another sign of the weakness which will lead to her final breakdown? In performances you have seen, which interpretation does each director choose?

A tormented soul

After Act 3 scene 4 we see little of Lady Macbeth as her husband continues on his trail of terror without her support. Presumably Shakespeare wished to maintain the focus on Macbeth but her absence also suggests the decline in their relationship. Without him needing her strength, there is nothing left for her to do but dwell on their deeds. Whatever strength she gained from the spirits ultimately cannot protect her from her conscience and she becomes mentally disturbed.

GRADE *BOOSTER*

Some discussion of the symbiotic element of the Macbeths' relationship - swapping roles and characteristics - would show your understanding of the dramatic structure of the play.

Ironically, she is now the one whose sleep is disrupted. Where at the start of the play her words invited darkness to conceal all evil-doings, now she is said to insist on a light by her bed at all times.

Key quotation

...Unnatural deeds
Do breed unnatural troubles: infected minds
To their deaf pillows will discharge their secrets.
(5.1 61–63)

After the sleep-walking scene, no more is seen of Lady Macbeth. However, her death is marked by screams shortly after this and it is later said she died at her own hand.

'Fiend-like queen'

Malcolm's final comment about Lady Macbeth ('fiend-like queen' 5.9 36) emphasises her evil nature and reminds the audience of the link between her and the weird sisters.

Build critical skills

The audience may form a more complex interpretation of Lady Macbeth's character. She may be pitied: she sells her soul to get the thing her husband most desires and he deserts her emotionally when she most needs his support. Does she break the mould of femininity as she at first requests? (See *Plot and structure* p. 17.) What is your view?

She is one of Shakespeare's strongest and most memorable female characters but you should remember that when Shakespeare wrote the play her part would have been played by a young boy actor.

The weird sisters

It is not quite accurate to discuss the 'characterisation' of the weird sisters as they are often not presented as human, but rather as manifestations of the forces of evil. However, they have such a powerful effect on the plot that they could hardly be called 'minor', so their powers and influence are described here.

They appear on stage in just three scenes: Act1 scene 1, Act 1 scene 3 and Act 4 scene 1. (Act 3 scene 5 with Hecate was most likely added to the play at a later date by another writer.) Nevertheless, these three scenes are critical to Macbeth's fate.

Shakespeare's decision to open the play with the short scene where the witches plan to meet Macbeth is dramatically very effective. It establishes a dark, evil atmosphere, while the reference to the names of their familiars, Graymalkin and Paddock, would have shown a contemporary audience beyond doubt that they are in league with the devil. They talk of a battle – so the immediate background of the play is of chaos, fighting and death.

The witches express themselves in a spell-like rhyme and rhythm with words that are riddles.

Most important of all, they want Macbeth – and they get him.

Temptation

The witches' love of mischief and the promises they make to Macbeth and Banquo are discussed in detail in *Plot and structure* (Act 1 scene 3) on pp. 14–16.

Do you think the effect this information will have on the two men is predictable? The witches promise Macbeth the crown, then immediately snatch it away by promising the succession to his best friend. It is bound to lead to trouble: the carnage that follows must delight these trouble-makers.

Pure evil

Ignoring Act 3 scene 5, as this is frequently cut from performances, the witches' final encounter follows Macbeth's traumatic experience with Banquo's ghost when he returns to gain reassurance about the future.

The spell they recite as they concoct their poisonous sounding potion would have reinforced beliefs about the power of witches in the seventeenth century, and still has enormous dramatic impact today.

Build critical skills

Some directors show the witches still present at the end of the play, an on-going threat to Malcolm's apparent restoration of order to Scotland. What would you choose to do?

Key quotation

For a charm of powerful trouble,
Like a hell-broth boil and bubble.
(4.1 18–19)

The greatest indicator of their evil intentions comes in the form of the three predictions made by the apparitions (see *Plot and structure* p. 26). The witches refer to these apparitions as 'our masters', so are these words meant to come straight from the devil himself? Here the witches really do seem to be 'the fiends that lie like truth', as Macbeth later calls them when he realises they have tricked him.

GRADE *BOOSTER*

If you have the opportunity to write about the witches for your exam task, referring to context, language and performed versions of the play should help you present a well-informed view.

King Duncan and his sons, Malcolm and Donalbain

King Duncan

If the witches symbolise the power of the devil, Shakespeare uses Duncan and his sons to represent God's power on earth. They represent *order* to the witches' *chaos*.

Duncan's first appearance shows him receiving news from the battlefield, where the Scottish army is holding off Norwegian invaders in league with Scottish traitors. He is full of praise and gratitude for the bravery of Macbeth and Banquo.

He is benevolent and caring: he sends for a surgeon for the wounded captain who has brought the news. He is judgemental too, punishing the traitor Thane of Cawdor by death and rewarding Macbeth with the title.

▲ Duncan meeting Macbeth in person.

Duncan next appears as he greets Macbeth in person. His greeting shows he is related to Macbeth:

> Oh valiant cousin!

(1.2 24)

There is irony throughout this scene as he expresses his regret about the death of the Thane of Cawdor.

We see him similarly taken in by Lady Macbeth when he arrives at Macbeth's castle. In most stage productions, he is never seen again, though the imagery in the descriptions of him after the murder, from both Macbeth and Macduff, indicate the brutality of his death and the enormity of the sin that caused it.

Key quotation

Confusion now hath made his masterpiece:
Most sacrilegious murder hath broke ope
The Lord's anointed temple and stole thence
The life o'th' building.
(2.3 59–62)

Build critical skills

How would you present Duncan on stage? The RSC (Nunn) production, symbolically, has him in shining white, a bearded God-like figure, an absolute contrast to the darkness and black costumes of most of the other characters, and certainly to the weird sisters whose early scenes are juxtaposed with Duncan's first appearance.

As he plans Banquo's murder, Macbeth still reflects on Duncan as a 'gracious' king (3.1 67). Macduff's comments to Malcolm all emphasise the holiness of Duncan and his queen:

> a most sainted King; The Queen…Oft'ner upon her knees than on her feet…

(4.3 109–110)

Malcolm

Malcolm is with Duncan at the camp while Macbeth fights. The Captain who brings the news is the very man who saved him from capture. It appears Malcolm is no more successful as a soldier than his father. Despite this his father still declares him heir to the throne, an act which presses forward Macbeth's thoughts about killing Duncan and Malcolm too.

45

Malcolm gains importance when Macduff visits him in England. This long and complex scene invites us to compare Malcolm with Macbeth and Duncan, and eventually shows Malcolm to be a morally impeccable man, the right choice to free Scotland from the tyranny of an evil king.

Key quotation

...I am yet

Unknown to woman; never was forsworn;

...At no time broke my faith...and delight

No less in truth than life. My first false speaking

Was this upon myself.

(4.3 125–131)

He assembles a combined force of English soldiers and Scots who desert Macbeth to fight alongside the rightful heir. He is presented as resourceful as his is the ingenious idea of cutting down the trees of Birnam Wood to use as camouflage. He sends Siward's troops into the castle first and he and Macduff follow on: he is clearly presented as more of a warrior king than his father.

He concludes the play with a model speech, restoring right and order to Scotland. Like Duncan, he punishes the bad and rewards the good.

...what needful else

That calls upon us, by the grace of Grace,

We will perform in measure, time and place.

(5.9 38–40)

Donalbain

Duncan's younger son disappears after the murder and never returns. His function is to show Duncan as the father of sons (as also are Banquo, Macduff and Siward) in contrast to Macbeth's childlessness. The reason he is not on stage at the end is less to do with Shakespeare's forgetfulness as the limited number of actors in the theatre company. The same actor who was Donalbain in Acts 1 and 2 might well have been playing the Doctor, Siward, or any other soldier by Act 5.

Banquo and his son, Fleance

At the start of the play Banquo is coupled with Macbeth as a great general and fearless soldier. Their characters quickly become distinct when they meet the witches. Macbeth is immediately intrigued by their words whereas Banquo is sceptical and speaks a prophetic warning to Macbeth.

GRADE BOOSTER

Just as Duncan and Malcolm's purpose is to contrast with Macbeth as king, so Banquo contrasts with him as a man. Observe carefully how Shakespeare reveals their opposing qualities as the play develops. Making effective links between oppositional characters will help increase your marks.

The major contrast between Banquo and Macbeth is his resistance to temptation. Like Macbeth, he dwells on the promise made to him, and like Macbeth, his thoughts turn to evil doing. He says that his dreams allow him 'cursed thoughts', but he calls upon 'merciful powers' to protect him rather than following through to sinful deeds.

Macbeth fears Banquo's goodness: his 'royalty of nature...dauntless temper...wisdom that does guide his valour'. More to the point, Macbeth wishes to ensure that Banquo's sons do not become his successors as king, and thus determines to eradicate both him and his son, Fleance.

Loyal to the king

After Duncan's murder, Banquo's suspicions are implied: '...I fight/ Of treasonous malice' but, ironically, he says nothing and attends Macbeth's coronation. James I claimed that he was descended from Banquo and therefore Shakespeare presents him positively to appeal to his patron.

However, it could also be argued that Banquo is flawed. Shakespeare uses soliloquy to allow him to share with the audience his thoughts that Macbeth used foul-play to make the witches' promise come true. However, he is shown to remain loyal to his new king and one-time friend, perhaps in the hope that he too might benefit. You might therefore say that Banquo is, in a way, seduced by the forces of evil. This interpretation is closer to the original *Holinshed's Chronicles* source material.

Banquo goes along with Macbeth's invitation to be chief guest at the banquet and pays with his life for his possible lack of integrity as Macbeth's hired killers ambush him and stab him to death.

GRADE BOOSTER

> Exploring different viewpoints about a character can gain you extra marks. It is one way of showing that you have thought deeply about alternative interpretations.

He does, however, assure the truth of the witches' promise – his best revenge on Macbeth – as he begs his son to save himself.

Build critical skills

What of Banquo's ghost? Does it make sense to discuss it as part of Banquo's revenge? Whether you would include Act 3 scene 4 in evaluating Banquo's character might depend upon how you interpret the ghost. Look again at *Context* p. 11 and then reach your conclusion.

Key quotation

...oftentimes, to win us to our harm,

The instruments of darkness tell us truths,

Win us with honest trifles, to betray's

In deepest consequence.

(1.3 122–125)

Key quotation

...by the verities on thee made good

May not they be my oracles as well

And set me up in hope?

(3.1 8–10)

Key quotation

Fly good Fleance!...

Thou may'st revenge – O slave!

(3.3 20–21)

Fleance

Fleance is not so much a character as another reminder of Macbeth's childless state. He is usually played by a child actor and thus evokes feelings of affection and sympathy from the audience. He is, like King Duncan's sons, a motherless child. Remember that the play displays an absence of women in a male-dominated society.

Fleance's main contribution is not so much to the plot as to the play's historical significance as he flees (like his name) to become the ancestor of the Stewart dynasty of kings, and James I.

Macduff, his wife and son

Macduff is similar to Banquo as a character, emerging after Duncan's death as the loyal courtier who is appalled to discover Duncan's murdered body. He has suspicions about Macbeth, but instead of keeping quiet and becoming a deferential courtier who could benefit from Macbeth's rule, he speaks out.

For example, in the aftermath of Duncan's murder he questions Macbeth's killing of the king's guards: 'Wherefore did you so?' Macduff's sparing words contrast with Macbeth's extravagant expression.

Macduff refuses to attend the coronation or the banquet and pays dearly for it. Macbeth acts on the words of the first apparition to 'Beware Macduff': Macduff's absence in England costs him his family and his entire household.

Macduff is already a positive figure to the audience for the love he shows for his country and the anguish he expresses when he fears that Malcolm may not be the saviour he hoped for. When news of his family's slaughter reaches him, he shows himself to be worthy of sympathy as a man, grappling with his grief as a husband and father before converting those feelings into fuel for his vengeance on Macbeth.

Macduff's most dramatic moment is when he puts paid to Macbeth's security and reveals the riddling half-truths the witches used to deceive him (see *Plot and structure* p. 33).

He fights for his country, his murdered king and his slaughtered family. He defeats Macbeth, cuts off his head – as was the custom with traitors – and hails Malcolm as the true King of Scotland.

Build critical skills

What is Shakespeare's point here? Ought Macduff to have put his country before his family? Was it sensible to leave his castle unguarded? Lady Macduff says he is a coward for running away from Scotland. What is your view?

Key quotation

Macduff was from his mother's womb

Untimely ripp'd.

(5.8 15–16)

GRADE *FOCUS*

Grade 5

Students will be aware of characters as having clear purposes in a text. They will select evidence from the text and discuss relevant supporting detail from performances. Their comment on language and structure will be clear and relevant. Discussion of qualities of character will be clear and precise and may begin to consider alternative interpretations.

Grade 8

Students will offer a more perceptive response to hidden meanings and show an ability to grasp irony and to explore alternative readings. Their comment on language and structure will include perceptive analysis. Characters will be seen to represent themes and ideas as well as being believable creations. Discussion of performances will be more detailed and demonstrate analytical qualities.

REVIEW YOUR LEARNING

1 What are the main ways Shakespeare presents characters to readers in the play?

2 How many female characters appear in the play? Who are they?

3 What are the names of the four fathers, and what main purpose do they have in the play?

4 Which 'characters' symbolise the opposition of good and evil, heaven and hell, order and chaos?

5 Who is described as '…too full o'the milk of human kindness?'

6 Who says these words and to whom are they speaking? 'New honours come upon him/Like our strange garments – cleave not to their mould.' What theme is being suggested by these lines?

7 Who says '…Unnatural deeds/Do breed unnatural troubles: infected minds/To their deaf pillows will discharge their secrets.' What are the circumstances in which the lines are spoken?

Answers on p. 110.

Themes

Target your thinking

- What are the main themes in *Macbeth*? (**AO1** and **AO3**)
- How do these themes relate to each other? (**AO1** and **AO3**)
- How do these themes relate to the characters? (**AO1**)
- How are themes reflected in the language and imagery of the play? (**AO2**)

A theme in a play is an idea or group of ideas that the playwright explores. There is no one way to define the themes in a work of literature, and in any interpretation of literary themes there will be some overlap. Here is a list of suggested themes in *Macbeth*:

- order and chaos
- ambition
- the supernatural
- darkness and light
- appearance and reality
- sickness and health

Notice how many of these themes are linked opposites. An overarching theme in *Macbeth* is the battle between good and evil. Shakespeare does far more than simply tell an exciting story in his plays: he refers to ideas and debates that his educated audience are already familiar with. He also tries to make these complex ideas accessible to all members of his audience.

Order and chaos

God's order

The idea of order following from the belief that God established an organised hierarchy for all creation was one which most of Shakespeare's audience accepted. This was seen as 'natural', and phrases in *Macbeth* about events being 'unnatural' or 'against nature' suggest that God's divine order has been disrupted.

Chaotic happenings on earth, for example, man-made events such as war, or destructive weather, reflect the chaos unleashed by evil.

Chaos

Macbeth begins with elements of disorder: treachery against the king, war, storms, the supernatural unleashed to cause further chaos. Macbeth, fuelled by unnatural desires of ambition, changes sides. (See 'Ambition' below.) He moves, in minutes, from fighting for order, supporting his king, to contemplating the destruction of order via the murder of the king.

Disorder is to be found in the witches' delight in evil doing, and in their riddling and paradoxical language. (See 'The supernatural' below.) Lady Macbeth contributes by throwing off her natural femininity, as defined by contemporary audiences, goading her husband into committing the ultimate sin of murdering God's representative on earth, and worse still, stealing the role for himself.

Chaos follows Duncan's death: freakish weather and bizarre animal behaviour. (See Act 2 scene 4.)

As Macbeth's reign of terror continues, Scotland's social order slides into chaos. Macbeth compounds his acts of disloyalty, having his one-time best friend murdered then moving on to kill innocent women and children.

The banquet scene (Act 3 scene 4) symbolises in miniature the descent from order to chaos. It begins in a ritualised and formal way, everyone seated according to their 'degrees', their social rank. Macbeth's behaviour, speaking with the murderer and later, when he sees Banquo's ghost, is chaotic. The banquet ends with Lady Macbeth frantically dismissing the guests 'not on the order of your going...go at once'.

Lady Macbeth's madness is a symbolic form of disorder. (See 'Sickness and health' on p. 58.)

Order restored

Malcolm represents order. He plays a strange game with Macduff in Act 4 scene 3 to test his loyalty, pretending to be more evil than Macbeth, not a fit person to rule in God's place. However, he then explains why he misrepresented himself and shows that he is the man for the job. His closing speech shows order restored to Scotland as evil is punished and good rewarded.

Ambition

The theme of ambition is in some ways linked to the theme of order. In Shakespeare's time many people retained the medieval idea that God put a person into a particular position in life and that was their 'natural' place in the hierarchy. To wish for more was unnatural. Macbeth's ambition to be king leads him to commit a number of murderous acts.

A tragic flaw

The fatal flaw of ambition in a once worthy, noble character is one of the factors that identifies the play as a tragedy. Macbeth is a tragic hero, brought down by this flaw of character.

Throughout the play, Shakespeare makes clear Macbeth's ambition to be king. The witches know of it, thus it is Macbeth they seek out, rather than Banquo. His reaction to their words is to want what they promise, whatever the cost, which may suggest that the witches speak only what is already in his thoughts (see *Characterisation* p. 37).

Encouraged by the immediate fulfilment of the promise that he will become Thane of Cawdor, Macbeth imagines means of attaining the crown which are 'against the use of nature'. 'Murder' which is as yet 'but fantastical' (Act 1 scene 3).

Without his in-built ambition, the witches would have been unable to influence his actions, just as they are shown to be unable to gain Banquo's trust. Furthermore, Lady Macbeth recognises this characteristic and she plays on it fully. She is well aware that she has the persuasive power to make Macbeth do whatever needs to be done.

Macbeth acknowledges his ambition in his first soliloquy as he enumerates the reasons why he cannot kill Duncan. The speech ends with these words:

> ...I have no spur
>
> To prick the sides of my intent, but only
>
> Vaulting ambition, which o'erleaps itself
>
> And falls on the other –
>
> (1.7 25–28)

Key quotation

...Thou wouldst be great – art not without ambition,

But without the illness should attend it.

(1.5 16–18)

Ironically, as he is about to complete this metaphor, imagining his ambition as a jumping horse which takes a tumble, the 'spur' to his ambition enters: Lady Macbeth.

She knows ambition is his weak point and she accuses him of being a coward because he will not act to get what he really wants.

She accuses him of raising her hopes by promising that she would be his 'partner in greatness'.

Key quotation

...Art thou afeard

To be the same in thine own act and valour,
As thou art in desire?
(1.7 39–41)

Build critical skills

Does Shakespeare imply that Lady Macbeth's motivation is selfish, or selfless? Does *she* want to be a 'partner in greatness', a queen, or does she want this solely for her husband's sake?

By the end of Act 1, they are both damned. We see how one murder leads to another as Macbeth attempts to secure the prize his ambition drew him to. His ambition does not stop at being king: he kills Banquo partly because he wants the succession to be his, even though he has no heir.

> No son of mine succeeding…

> For Banquo's issue have I filed my mind

> (3.1 65–66)

He rules by fear to hold on to what he has wrongly achieved, returning to the witches to reassure himself that he is secure, and killing Macduff's family just because he can.

Lady Macbeth's disappointment is clear in one brief soliloquy which foreshadows her descent into madness.

> …Nought's had, all's spent,

> Where our desire is got without content.

> 'Tis safer to be that which we destroy

> Than by destruction dwell in doubtful joy.

> (3.2 4–7)

Macbeth's words echo these feelings of pointlessness, for example, his lack of satisfaction with the way his life has turned out (Act 5 scene 3), and reflection on his feelings when Lady Macbeth dies (Act 5 scene 5).

Key quotation

…a tale
Told by an idiot, full of sound and fury,
Signifying nothing.
(5.5 25–27)

Build critical skills

Is Shakespeare suggesting that ambition is inherently evil, or is the point that committing evil deeds in the pursuit of ambition will lead to punishment? The play does not give an answer. Only you can decide.

The supernatural

Today, as in Shakespeare's time, stories with a supernatural element that send chills down the spine are popular. The inclusion of both witchcraft and a ghost was a good way to get less educated members of the audience hooked. James I's terror of witches and his knowledge about them (see *Context* p. 10) would also make this interesting for members of his court and other more educated viewers.

An intriguing aspect of the supernatural characters is the scope for a wide range of interpretation. In this they link closely with the theme of appearance and reality. At the time of Shakespeare's writing there was less understanding of science and rationality. Witchcraft was an accepted explanation of why crops failed or animals caught diseases. Most of Shakespeare's audience would have taken the witches literally.

Modern productions may interpret the supernatural element in a psychoanalytical way. For example, it is possible to interpret the dagger as a hallucination caused by guilt, as is the spot of blood Lady Macbeth cannot wash off her hands. It could also be argued that Banquo's ghost and the apparitions are products of Macbeth's diseased mind.

> **GRADE BOOSTER**
>
> A psychoanalytical reading might make more sense to a modern audience where many have neither religious beliefs nor a belief in ghosts. As far as the play goes, it makes for better drama if the witches and the ghost are believed to real - suspension of disbelief is what drama is all about. Debating this effectively could gain you a high grade in a written response about this theme.

Darkness and light

Macbeth is a dark play, in its settings, its events and its language. The darkness is symbolic of evil, while light symbolises good, so this theme is closely linked with the others.

Darkness

The action opens on a bleak, dark note — a suitable setting for the witches. They describe the 'fog and filthy air' and they are accompanied by thunder and lightning. A similar setting provides a menacing atmosphere both times Macbeth speaks with the witches.

Much of the play takes place inside Macbeth's castle, a place where Shakespeare shows us both Macbeth and Lady Macbeth inviting darkness in, and which is explicitly compared with hell on several occasions.

The evil deeds of the play take place in the dark of night, and this is repeatedly mentioned in the dialogue. Banquo and Fleance remark on

Key quotation

...Come thick night, And pall thee in the dunnest smoke of hell —...
(1.5 48–49)

the moonless, starless night that is the background to Duncan's murder. Darkness remains as the sun fails to rise the following day.

...dark night strangles the travelling lamp...

darkness does the face of earth entomb...

(2.4 7–9)

Macbeth's words set the scene for the murder of Banquo as he describes the end of the day. Descriptions like this evoke a twilight world where good and evil stand in the balance against each other. Banquo's murder takes place in darkness as the lantern is put out in the struggle. The banquet ends as daylight breaks after a night of torment.

Light

Mentions of light are less frequent in the play. King Duncan is associated with light: early on he names Malcolm as his heir and promises that, in the future:

signs of nobleness, like stars shall shine

On all deservers.

(1.4 41–42)

Arriving at Macbeth's castle, Duncan does not sense the evil within, instead commenting on the pleasantness of the setting and the sweetness of the air. Banquo's comment about the 'martlets' is ironic (Act 1 scene 6), reminding us that house-martins often nest in church buildings.

Act 4 scene 3 is the only scene outside the Scottish setting, and the mentions of 'this good King' connect Edward with heaven, sanctity and virtue. Malcolm ends the scene by asking for help from the English army to bring light back to Scotland.

...Receive what cheer you may:

The night is long that never finds the day.

(4.3 242–243)

Although Lady Macbeth called upon darkness to hide her deeds, she brings light back into the castle when her madness leaves her afraid of the dark. She carries a lighted candle and her gentlewoman reports that:

She has light by her continually –'tis her command.

(5.1 19–20)

(There is more information relevant to this theme in *Language, style and analysis* on pp. 64–65.)

Key quotation

...*Light thickens; and the crow*

Makes wings to the rooky wood.

Good things of day begin to droop and drowse,

Whiles night's black agents to their preys do rouse.

(3.2 50–53)

Build critical skills

In stage productions, lighting and white costumes often set these scenes apart from the darkness of the rest of the play. Watch as many as you can and decide how you would symbolise this theme in a stage or film adaptation.

Appearance and reality

Yet another of the oppositions which Shakespeare investigates (and which is linked to the themes above) is how what *appears* may actually contrast with reality. This theme involves a range of ideas: deception, concealment, equivocation, paradox, clothing and disguise, and is reflected again and again in the language and imagery of the play.

Paradox

From the opening scene this theme is evident – the witches mention that the battle will be both 'lost' and 'won', in the sense that any conflict will have both winners and losers, then chant:

> Fair is foul, and foul is fair!

> (1.1 12)

a paradoxical line mirrored by Macbeth's first words:

> So foul and fair a day I have not seen.

> (1.3 36)

The witches seem to be women, but as Banquo comments, they have beards. He says their words 'sound so fair', yet Macbeth 'seem[s] to fear' them. 'Seems' quickly becomes a word which draws the audience to attention: how things seem in *Macbeth*, is rarely what they truly are.

Deceit and equivocation

The witches' initial promises come true, but do not bring the joy they seemed to offer. The three apparitions in Act 4 scene 1 speak words which seem to offer Macbeth rock-solid security, yet turn out to be

> …th'equivocation of the fiend

> That lies like truth.

> (5.5 42–43)

Yet did Macbeth really expect the devil to tell the honest truth? Right at the start, Banquo warns him about misplacing his trust (see *Plot and structure*, Act 1 scene 3, pp. 14–15). After all, the devil has something of a track record for tempting humanity with lying words.

Outward show

Duncan talks about how he was misled by the appearance of the original Thane of Cawdor. Perhaps he should not have been so trusting, since he is quickly misled by the new one, and by the wife of the new one as well.

Key quotation

There's no art
To find the mind's
construction in the face.
(1.4 11–12)

A key image linking with this theme is the advice Lady Macbeth gives to her husband as they plot Duncan's death.

> …look like th'innocent flower
>
> But be the serpent under't.
>
> (1.5 63–64)

In addition to concealing their thoughts and plans, the Macbeths repeatedly ask for darkness to conceal their deeds from the eyes of men and of God himself. (See 'Darkness and Light' above.) It is almost as though they (particularly Lady Macbeth) believe that what is not explicitly said, or seen, or heard, did not happen and will have no consequences. This moral blindness comes back to haunt Lady Macbeth later in the play.

Borrowed robes

Clothing is another kind of appearance – a cover up for reality – used thematically in the play. Macbeth wears 'borrowed robes' – the full regalia of the king, including crown and sceptre, all the symbols of kingly power. He might look like a king, but in the eyes of God he is not one.

By the end of the play, one of the insults applied to Macbeth echoes this image.

> …Now does he feel his title
>
> Hang loose upon him, like a giant's robe
>
> Upon a dwarfish thief.
>
> (5.2 20–22)

Illusions

See 'The supernatural' (pp. 53–54) for discussion of things that appear to be real, yet may be imaginary: the dagger, the ghost, the apparitions. Related to this theme, also consider Malcolm's lies about himself in Act 4 scene 3. The banquet in Act 3 scene 4 is also not the occasion it appears on the surface.

The underlying message

On an obvious level, Shakespeare is warning us to be wary of being taken in by superficial appearance, particularly when it offers tempting rewards. On a deeper level, there is a depth of questioning about old 'truths' which new ideas of the seventeenth century threw into doubt. For example, in medieval times, many believed that a beautiful face showed a person's moral goodness.

Sickness and health

Just as goodness is connected with light and evil with dark, the good kings – Duncan, Edward and ultimately Malcolm – are linked with life, health and growth, while Macbeth is linked with sickness and death.

At the start and end of the play, both Duncan and Malcolm speak very similar words:

Duncan:

I have begun to plant thee, and will labour

To make thee full of growing.

(1.4 28–29)

Malcolm:

...What's more to do,

Which would be planted newly with the time,

As calling home our exiled friend abroad...

(5.9 31–33)

Their words suggest they look after the growth and health of Scottish society as a whole, not just of individuals.

King Edward is described as having the power to cure disease – a 'healing benediction' – which he is able to pass on to his royal heirs, including James I.

Macbeth, quite the opposite, is associated with sickness, both of body and mind, from the outset. When he meets the witches, Banquo wonders whether the pair of them have 'eaten of the insane root/That takes the reason prisoner' (Act 3 scene 1) – a reference to a poison, like hemlock.

After Duncan's murder, Lady Macbeth interrupts Macbeth's ramblings about murdering sleep – the great 'balm of hurt minds' – by telling him not to think 'so brain-sickly' (Act 2 scene 2). Ironically she is the one who becomes insane.

As the action progresses, Macbeth's tyrannical rule is seen as affecting the health of 'our suffering country' (Act 3 scene 6). Macduff describes Scotland to Malcolm as injured and bleeding – 'and each new day a gash/ Is added to her wounds' – and Malcolm speaks of curing the nation with 'medicines of our great revenge' (Act 4 scene 3).

Macbeth suggests that the Doctor who cannot find a cure for his wife might be able to diagnose and cure his country. In fact it takes Macbeth's death to restore Scotland to health.

Build critical skills

Sleep, or the lack of it, is mentioned so frequently that it could be considered a theme in its own right. Remind yourself of the connections made between sleep and death in Act 2 scene 2 and Act 3 scene 2.

Key quotation

...cast

The water of my land, find her disease,

And purge it to a sound and pristine health...

(5.3 51–53)

GRADE *FOCUS*

Grade 5

Students will be able to identify specific themes and explain in a relevant manner how some characters illustrate aspects of a theme. They will develop a sound personal response and may be able to explain how some aspects of the play in performance reflect the themes.

Grade 8

Students will be able to sustain discussion about how a range of characters and events illustrate aspects of a theme. They will analyse perceptively the use of language and imagery to illustrate the themes and will also consider how the play can be interpreted in performance to highlight themes, developing a convincing and informed personal opinion.

REVIEW YOUR LEARNING

1 What is a theme?

2 Which six main themes are identified in this guide?

3 Which theme appears to give the greatest insight into Macbeth and Lady Macbeth's characters?

4 Who is presented as the main example of the theme of appearance and reality?

5 Which theme is most closely associated with the historical context of the play?

6 Which three themes are most obviously reflected in the play's imagery?

7 Which theme might lead us to judge Macbeth to be a tragic hero?

8 Do you think the themes of the play are as relevant for a modern audience as they might have been when Shakespeare wrote the play in the early seventeenth century?

Answers on p. 111.

Language, style and analysis

Target your thinking

- What features do the terms 'language' and 'style' refer to? (**AO2**)
- What is a soliloquy? (**AO2**)
- What use does Shakespeare make of verse and prose? (**AO2** and **AO3**)
- How does Shakespeare use imagery and symbolism? (**AO2**)
- What other devices are used in the play? (**AO2**)

When you write about style, you are showing that you understand that the playwright has numerous choices. Your job as a literary critic – because that is what you are when you write your essay – is to identify what choices Shakespeare has made and to assess how effective they are.

The list below gives some of the main features covered by the word 'style'. Shakespeare has made choices about all of them:

- **dialogue** (the words spoken by the actors – which may be conversation between two or more characters, or may be *soliloquy*) – how it is used to tell the story, to reveal character or to create atmosphere
- **verse** and **prose** – how the dialogue is patterned
- **imagery** – the way in which the writer uses word pictures: techniques such as metaphor, simile and personification
- **symbolism** – how abstract ideas can be explored through objects/concepts
- **irony** and **dramatic irony**

GRADE *BOOSTER*

Shakespeare did not write his plays to be read. They are meant to be acted on stage. Always bear in mind the importance of stagecraft when answering your question in the examination.

Dialogue

When you read a play, what you see is the dialogue which would be spoken on stage. These words lead you through the narrative and allow you to gain an understanding of the characters. Once the dialogue is performed, on stage or in a film, visual elements such as costume, tone of voice, facial expression and actions add to the information you might interpret.

Let us consider how dialogue works as conversation in just one scene of the play. This will show you how to comment in detail on the effects of an extract of the play which includes a range of dialogue.

Re-read Act 4 scene 2, the scene where Macduff's family are slaughtered. This is the only scene where these characters (except for Ross) appear.

Dialogue allows the audience to form a clear impression of them in a short time.

There is clever **juxtaposition** of scenes: the setting changes from the menace of the witches and Macbeth's bloody intentions to the home of Macduff. Lady Macduff speaks to Ross. Her words emphasise how vulnerable her family is. She asks the reason for her husband's desertion of the family: he has placed them in danger by leaving them unprotected. She gains sympathy when she says simply 'he loves us not'.

She communicates anger and amazement at her husband's actions, saying that even a wren will protect its young in the nest. Ross defends Macduff but agrees that 'cruel are the times'. He comforts her by reminding her that when things reach rock bottom, they must improve.

> Things at the worse will cease, or else climb upward
>
> To what they were before.
>
> (4.2 24–25)

Shakespeare uses Ross to remind us of the structure of a tragedy (see *Plot and structure* p. 28).

He implies that he may disgrace himself by crying, or damage her reputation by being there alone with her, if he stays longer.

There is a **subtext** here to work out: he obviously admires Macduff, who seems to be a relation, since he calls Lady Macduff 'cos' (cousin) but his actions imply that the safest course is loyalty to Macbeth, not association with someone who has got on the wrong side of the tyrant.

Lady Macduff then turns her attention to her son, who would be played by a child actor. Her words show her to be an affectionate mother, witty and strong for her child, while he is portrayed as a clever and brave little boy, honest in his innocence.

She asks the boy how he will cope without a father and he innocently replies that he can fend for himself as the birds can. His words reflect the earlier **imagery** about how wrens protect their fledglings and **foreshadow** the murderer calling him an 'egg' at the end of the scene.

Lady Macduff's comments about buying new husbands at market would bring smiles to the faces of the audience, despite the serious subtext of danger in many of their words. The boy turns Lady Macduff's words back on her, saying his father is not dead. The audience knows that, though the father is still alive, this little family will soon not be, adding to the **tension** and the **pathos** of this scene. A seventeenth-century audience would have felt the same terror as the scene evokes today. The boy asks if his father was a traitor and speaks words of innocent wisdom when he says that there are enough 'liars and swearers to hang all the honest men'. Yes – and some are on the way at this moment!

Key quotation

I am in this earthly world where to do harm

Is often laudable, to do good sometime

Accounted dangerous folly.

(4.2 72–74)

A messenger enters – a **dramatic device**, not a real character, a means of providing information to **promote the plot**. He warns Lady Macduff of approaching danger and tells her to take her children and leave. Tension mounts further as she says she has nowhere to go. Shakespeare again reminds us of the innocence and vulnerability of the family with no husband and father to protect them. The messenger runs away in fear.

An unspecified number of hired killers enter, though only one speaks. These are not real, rounded characters, but they contribute to the subtext by making us consider what kind of society produces and makes use of callous killers like these.

The murderer asks where Macduff is, then justifies his brutal actions by calling him a traitor. The child shows himself to be as brave as his father, standing up to the attackers and contradicting these words. He is killed right there in front of the audience, one of the most shocking acts of brutality in the play. He reminds us of Banquo as his final words aim to save his mother's life.

Build critical skills

This is a horrible moment on stage. Look at different interpretations to see how the child's murder is portrayed. The line 'He has killed me mother' is hard to deliver on stage: it often makes the audience laugh, though if the death is conducted as a surprise, it can be horrific. Similarly the fate of Lady Macduff, her final screams ringing in the audience's ears. How do you react to the end of this scene?

Soliloquies and asides

Not all dialogue is shared *between* the characters on stage. Playwrights use stylised means of letting us know what a character is thinking where the words they speak are not for other actors, but for the audience. A **soliloquy** is a speech spoken by an actor alone on stage and it was an accepted convention at the time when the play was written. Shakespeare's audience would have understood that it was a true and honest reflection of the character's state of mind at that time. Soliloquies are, therefore, crucial for understanding the character in question.

Macbeth speaks three true soliloquies:

- Act 1 scene 7, where he reflects on his reservations about killing Duncan (see *Plot and structure* p. 18)
- Act 2 scene 1, where he sees the dagger (see *Plot and structure* pp. 19–20)
- Act 3 scene 1, where he justifies killing Banquo (see *Plot and structure* p. 23)

These are not the only occasions when Macbeth speaks his thoughts aloud. On other occasions he reveals a great deal to the audience in **asides** – speeches made in the presence of other characters but which they are not meant to hear. The most important of these are:

- Act 1 scene 3, after he has heard the witches' promises (see *Plot and structure* p. 16)
- Act 4 scene 1, after he has seen the apparitions (see *Plot and structure* p. 26)
- Act 5 scene 5, after Lady Macbeth's death (see *Plot and structure* p. 31)

Other characters also speak soliloquies. For example, Lady Macbeth is alone for most of Act 1 scene 5, when she receives Macbeth's letter, and, more briefly, alone and unhappy in Act 3 scene 2. Banquo also reveals his suspicions of Macbeth in a soliloquy in Act 3 scene 1.

Verse and prose

The language used in Shakespeare's plays is not the sort of language you hear today. Four hundred years ago English was not spoken as it is now, so some vocabulary will be unfamiliar to you. Furthermore, stylised theatrical conventions that Shakespeare followed prescribe that much of the time the characters speak in **poetry** (more accurately referred to as **blank verse**), lines with a particular rhythm and sometimes with rhyme. Speeches also include complex imagery (see below).

Characters higher in rank, such as the Macbeths, anyone of royal or noble blood, or anyone speaking in a particularly dramatic way will speak in blank verse. This gives the impression that these characters are more important.

Blank verse

When human characters speak in verse, it follows a pattern used by many playwrights of Shakespeare's time: the lines are similar in length and contain about **ten syllables**. In his verse, Shakespeare uses **iambic pentameter** which consists of five soft beats and five hard beats. For instance:

    – / – / – / – / – /

  So foul and fair a day I have not seen.

Each soft beat is followed immediately by a hard beat. This rhythm pattern with no rhyme is called **blank verse**.

Although actors do not emphasise the soft and hard beats when they speak, the rhythm can reveal a great deal about the state of mind of a character.

> ### Build critical skills
>
> In film adaptations today there are more **naturalistic** methods of communicating characters' thoughts to the viewer. How could speeches direct to the audience be presented on screen?

GRADE **BOOSTER**

Sharing iambic pentameter lines between speakers is a technique called **stichomythia**. It is often used to create tension. An excellent example comes just after Duncan's murder (Act 2 scene 2 line 16 onwards), where the jumpy exchanges between the Macbeths show how on edge they are. Analysing language in detail like this will help you reach top grades.

Prose

Prose is normal speech with no pattern of rhythm or rhyme. It is spoken by characters lower in rank, for example, servants such as the Porter in Act 2 scene 3. It is also spoken *to* lower rank characters, as when Macbeth addresses the murderers in Act 3 scene 1.

You may also notice that Lady Macbeth speaks in prose in two scenes. The first time is when she reads aloud Macbeth's letter about the witches in Act 1 scene 5, so that it is clear to the audience which are his words and which are hers. The second time is in Act 5 scene 1, to reflect the disturbed state of her mind and her chaotic thoughts.

Imagery

Imagery refers to the kind of word pictures a writer creates to help us imagine what is being described. Imagery is closely linked with the themes of the play, so it will be useful to read these sections together. There are three main kinds of imagery used throughout *Macbeth*:

- **simile** – when one thing is compared with another, using 'like' or 'as'
- **metaphor** – when something is described as if it actually is something else
- **personification** – when something that is not human is given human characteristics

Examples of each kind of image are explained in detail below.

Images of darkness and light

Light and dark are used as metaphors for good and evil (see *Themes* pp. 54–55). Some metaphors refer to nocturnal animals:

…Ere the bat hath flown

His cloistered flight; ere to black Hecate's summons

The shard-borne beetle, with his drowsy hums,

Hath rung night's yawning peal…

(3.2 40–43)

Here Shakespeare sets the scene for Banquo's murder. The bat is pictured flying through the arches of an old monastery, the hum of the beetle's scaly wings is compared to the tolling of the evening church bell.

Night is personified as something that can blind the light of day, linking it with the theme of appearance and reality (see *Themes* pp. 56–57). In the same speech, Macbeth uses the imperative:

> ...Come seeling Night,
>
> Scarf up the tender eye of pitiful day,
>
> And, with thy bloody and invisible hand,
>
> Cancel and tear to pieces that great bond
>
> Which keeps me pale!
>
> (3.2 46–50)

Day is personified as having eyes to see and feelings of pity. Night is told to blindfold day and, with an unseen hand, tear up the life of Banquo.

Religious imagery

The play is full of imagery concerned with heaven and hell. When Macbeth reflects on the many reasons for not killing Duncan, Shakespeare emphasises Duncan's goodness using similes:

> ...his virtues
>
> Will plead like angels, trumpet-tongued...
>
> And pity, like a naked new-born babe striding the blast,
>
> Or heaven's cherubin...
>
> Shall blow the horrid deed in every eye.
>
> (1.7 18–24)

This creates a picture of angels singing out Duncan's saintliness, and the defencelessness of the baby, or of the heavenly cherubs who would join the storm of protest against such an evil deed.

In contrast, Shakespeare's other characters often refer to Macbeth and Lady Macbeth using language that connects the couple with hell. Lady Macbeth is dismissed by Malcolm as a 'fiend-like queen', whereas both Malcolm and Macduff compare Macbeth with the devil himself:

> Not in the legions
>
> Of horrid hell can come a devil more damned
>
> In evils to top Macbeth.
>
> (4.3 55–57)

Imagery of blood and milk

Macbeth is associated with blood. Blood is in his thoughts long before his hands are stained with Duncan's blood, and it becomes a river in his imagination (See *Characterisation* p. 38).

> …his brandished steel…smoked with bloody execution

(1.2 17–18)

> Except they meant to bathe in reeking wounds…

(1.2 39)

After Banquo's murder, there is no stopping it.

> It will have blood, they say, blood will have blood.

(3.4 122)

There is also an association of blood with guilt, which Lady Macbeth's endless hand-washing at the end of the play underlines.

Milk is nurturing, life-giving, as seen in Lady Macbeth's reference to breast-feeding (1.7 54–55). Note that she asks the spirits to 'take my milk for gall' (1.5 46) as she casts off her femininity.

Build critical skills

How many images can you find that connect blood with water? For example, no amount of water can wash the soul clean – and the image of blood staining the sea, or flowing in rivers symbolises the guilt caused by shedding blood.

Disease imagery

Metaphors of disease link with the themes of sickness and health (see *Themes* p. 58) and order and chaos (see *Themes* pp. 50–51).

Key quotation

Though the treasure
Of nature's germens tumble all together
Even till destruction sicken! – answer me
To what I ask you.
(4.1 57–60)

The witches infect Macbeth with their evil and this is a disease which spreads from him to the country, so Shakespeare could be suggesting that the whole state of Scotland becomes sick. In the seventeenth century, contagious and incurable diseases like the plague were very much feared.

Imagery about clothing

This is discussed as an aspect of the theme of appearance and reality (see *Themes* pp. 56–57). Shakespeare includes many metaphors about 'borrowed' clothes, reflecting Macbeth's wrongful acquisition of the role of king.

Animal imagery

References to animals occur throughout, from the witches' familiars to the imagined creatures of the night in the metaphors discussed above. Shakespeare has Macduff comparing Macbeth to a bird of prey and a dog, while Lady Macbeth implies that he is a 'beast' as opposed to a man when he shows fear about killing Duncan in Act 1 scene 7.

Snakes are also linked with religious imagery, for example, the reference to the devil in the Garden of Eden (see *Plot and structure* p. 18).

Imagery about time

One aspect of time, the future, is central to the plot of *Macbeth* as encapsulated by the witches' predictions in Act 1 scene 3 and in Act 4 scene 1. Banquo asks the witches:

> If you can look into the seeds of time,
>
> And say which grain will grow, and which will not,
>
> Speak then to me.
>
> (1.3 56–58)

Shakespeare's metaphor connects time with images concerned with planting and growth (see *Themes* p. 58) and with Macbeth's comment about 'nature's germens' above.

> **GRADE** *BOOSTER*
>
> ```
> Merely mentioning that Shakespeare uses devices such
> as imagery or symbolism will not gain you a good
> mark. Always show the examiner that you understand
> how the device works and the effect it creates for
> the audience.
> ```

Symbolism

A **symbol** is something that the playwright uses consistently to represent or 'stand for' something else. There is room for personal interpretation here: not all critics interpret a symbol in exactly the same way. Some of the recurring images discussed above are used as symbols: contrasts of light and dark, order and chaos, health and disease can all symbolise good and evil.

Symbols of power

Regalia connected with kingship symbolise the power of the role: the crown, the sceptre and the orb. On stage, these symbols would be visually reinforced. Macbeth refers to them as he dwells on the witches' promise to Banquo.

Build critical skills

At one point Macbeth tells Lady Macbeth that his mind is 'full of scorpions' (3.2 36). What kind of creature is a scorpion? What do you think this metaphor reveals about Macbeth's mental state?

Build critical skills

Time is often personified as though it has an intelligence and influence on people. How many examples of this can you find in the play?

Key quotation

Upon my head they placed a fruitless crown,

And put a barren sceptre in my gripe…

(3.1 62–63)

Animal symbolism

One image which recurs is that of the bird of prey. When the Captain is asked whether a surge of fresh troops 'dismayed' Macbeth and Banquo, he replies ironically:

Yes, as sparrows eagles…

(1.2 35)

associating Macbeth with the noble eagle, 'king' of the birds.

Later, the topsy-turvy events after Duncan's death include:

A falcon, towering in her pride of place,

Was by a mousing owl hawked at and killed.

(2.4 12–13)

The falcon is the nobler bird, representing Duncan, while the owl is Macbeth.

Later still, Lady Macduff and her son are linked with birds as she discusses her husband's departure and then how her son would live without a father (see p. 61).

…the poor wren,

The most diminutive of birds, will fight,

Her young ones in her nest, against the owl.

(4.2 9–11)

When Macduff is told of his family's death, we see symbolised Macbeth's fall from noble eagle to vicious hellish predator on helpless prey.

Key quotation

…O hell-kite! – All?

What, all my pretty chickens, and their dam,

At one fell-swoop?

(4.3 219–221)

Irony and dramatic irony

Irony occurs frequently in the play, one example being the words of Lady Macduff as she speaks to her son (see p. 61). Duncan's innocence and trusting nature also leads to ironic words, as he talks of his trust in the Thane of Cawdor in Act 1 scene 4 (see p. 16) and in Act 1 scene 6 when he praises Macbeth's castle and his hostess, thanking her for the trouble she has put into preparing for his visit (see p. 18).

Dramatic irony puts the audience one step ahead of the characters on stage. For example, when the Porter in Act 2 scene 3 imagines himself working at the gates of hell, there is more truth there than he realises. Also, when Ross brings Macduff the appalling news about his family, he is unable to say the words, and pronounces that they were '…well at peace when I did leave'em' (4.3 181).

GRADE BOOSTER

Analysis of ironic or dramatically ironic moments in the play and the correct application of such terminology will help you gain marks.

Finally, the audience realises long before Macbeth that the witches' promises in Act 4 scene 1 are tricks. As soon as the British army cut down the trees in Act 5 scene 4, we anticipate Macbeth's reaction and try to work out how Macbeth's killer will not be born of a woman. Macduff's revelation that he was born by caesarean section usually comes as a surprise.

Repetition

Themes are not only reflected by use of imagery, but sometimes by the frequent use of single words. In *Macbeth*, unsurprisingly, one of the most frequently occurring words is 'blood', or 'bloody'. The words 'done' and 'undone' are used to describe acts and consequences.

Opposite words like 'won', 'lost', 'fair', 'foul' are first used together in a paradoxical way by the witches, but turn up again in other speeches. The word 'equivocate' is used in several different places, underlining the misleading nature of the witches' words. Words connected with Christianity, such as 'heaven' and 'hell', 'man' and 'beast', 'natural' and 'unnatural', remind us of God's ordering of the universe.

Build critical skills

Significant words like these are sometimes given extra emphasis by alliteration with similar sounding words: 'fear' and 'fair', for example, in Act 1 scene 3. Can you find other examples of this technique?

Comic relief

For discussion of **comic relief** in Act 2 scene 3, see *Plot and structure* p. 21.

REVIEW YOUR LEARNING

1 How is dialogue used to reveal characters to the reader/audience?

2 What is a soliloquy? How does Shakespeare use these to develop a character?

3 Which characters in the play speak in prose and which in poetry, and why?

4 What is stichomythia and how is it used in *Macbeth*?

5 Name two techniques used to introduce humour to the play.

6 Select an example of a metaphor linked with a particular theme and explain its effect.

7 What use does Shakespeare make of birds of prey as symbols?

8 What is dramatic irony? Give an example from *Macbeth*.

Answers on pp. 111–112.

GRADE *FOCUS*

Grade 5

Students will be able to identify a range of aspects of language and structure, for example, explaining how imagery communicates something about a character or a theme. They will comment clearly on how dialogue develops plot and character, with relevant evidence selected from the text. Literary terminology will be used with clarity.

Grade 8

Students will offer a perceptive and sustained appreciation of a variety of features of language and structure to achieve grade 8. They will need to show an increasingly sophisticated evaluation and analysis of evidence to reach the highest grades. Literary critical terminology will be used with precision.

Tackling the exams

Target your thinking

- What sorts of questions will you have to answer?
- What is the best way to plan and structure your answer?
- How can you improve your grade?
- What do you have to do to achieve the highest grade?

Your response to a question on Macbeth will be assessed in a 'closed book' English Literature examination, which means that you are not allowed to take copies of the text into the examination room. Different examination boards will test you in slightly different ways, so it is vital that you know on which paper the Shakespeare question will appear and the sort of question you will be answering, so that you can be well-prepared on the day of the examination.

Whichever exam board you are following, the table opposite explains which paper and section the question appears in and gives you information about the sort of question you will face and how you will be assessed.

Marking

The marking of your responses varies according to the board your school or you have chosen. Each exam board will have a slightly different mark scheme, consisting of a ladder of grades. The marks you achieve in each part of the examination will be converted to your final overall grade. Grades are numbered from 1–9, with 9 being the highest.

It is important that you familiarise yourself with the relevant mark scheme(s) for your examination. After all, how can you do well unless you know exactly what is required?

Assessment Objectives for individual assessments are explained in the next section of the guide (see p. 79).

Approaching the examination question

First impressions

First read the whole question and make sure you understand *exactly* what it requires you to do. It is very easy in the highly pressured atmosphere of the examination room to misread a question and this can be disastrous. Under no circumstances should you try to twist the question to the one that you have spent hours revising or the one that you answered brilliantly in your mock exam.

Exam board	AQA	Edexcel	OCR	Eduqas
Paper/section	Paper 1 Section A	Paper 1 Section A	Paper 2 Section B	Paper 1 Section A
Type of question	Extract-based question requiring a response to an aspect of the extract and a response to **the same/similar** aspect in the **play as a whole.**	Two-part question: **Part (a):** extract-based question requiring close response to language. **Part (b):** question requiring a response about a **linked theme** or idea **elsewhere in the play.**	*Either* an extract-based question requiring a response to an aspect of the extract and **the same** aspect in the **play as a whole.** *Or* an essay question requiring a response to the **play as a whole.**	Two-part question: **Part (a):** extract-based question requiring a response to an aspect of the extract. **Part (b):** essay response to a different aspect in the **play as a whole.**
Closed book?	Yes	Yes	Yes	Yes
Choice of question?	No	No	Yes – answer one question from a choice of two.	No
Paper and section length	**Paper 1:** 1 hour 45 minutes **Section A:** approximately 50 minutes	**Paper 1:** 1 hour 45 minutes **Section A:** approximately 55 minutes	**Paper 2:** 2 hours **Section B:** 45 minutes	**Paper 1:** 2 hours **Section A:** approximately 1 hour – 20 minutes on extract task, 40 minutes on essay
% of whole grade	20% Literature grade	25% Literature grade	25% Literature grade	20% Literature grade
AOs assessed	AO1: 12 marks AO2: 12 marks AO3: 6 marks AO4: 4 marks **Total = 34 marks**	**Part (a):** AO2 only: 20 marks **Part (b):** AO1: 15 marks AO3: 5 marks **Total = 40 marks**	AO1: 16 marks AO2: 18 marks AO3: 4 marks AO4: 2 marks **Total = 40 marks**	**Part (a):** AO1: 7½ marks AO2: 7½ marks **Part (b):** AO1: 10 marks AO2: 10 marks AO4: 5 marks **Total = 40 marks**
Is AO4 (SPaG) assessed in this section?	Yes	No	Yes	Yes – in Part (b) only

Are you being asked to think about how a character or theme is presented or is the question focused more on exploring relationships, or attitudes? Make sure you know so that you are able to sustain your focus as you write.

As you can see from the table on p. 71, all the exam boards offer *Macbeth* as a text and all offer an extract-based question. However, the wording and format of the questions are slightly different for each board. The extract will be linked to one or two tasks for you to complete.

As a starting point, you may wish to underline key words in the question, such as 'how' to remind you to write about methods, and other words which you feel will help you to focus on answering the question you are being asked.

Below you can see examples of the question types from each examination board which have been annotated by students in this way.

AQA

Starting with this speech, <u>how far</u> do you do think Shakespeare presents <u>Lady Macbeth</u> as a <u>strong</u> and <u>influential</u> female character?

Write about:

- <u>how</u> Shakespeare presents Lady Macbeth in <u>this speech</u>
- <u>how</u> Shakespeare presents Lady Macbeth in the <u>play as a whole</u>

Edexcel

(a) Explore <u>how Shakespeare presents</u> <u>Lady Macbeth's feelings</u> in this extract.

Give <u>examples from the extract</u> to support your ideas.

(b) In this extract, <u>Lady Macbeth</u> talks about her desire to <u>manipulate Macbeth's</u> actions.

Explain the importance of <u>manipulation elsewhere</u> in the play.

In your answer you must consider:

- when others are <u>manipulating</u>, or <u>being manipulated</u>
- the reasons why <u>manipulation</u> is important to <u>events</u> in the play

You should refer to the <u>context </u>of the play in your answer.

OCR

EITHER

Explore the <u>changing relationship</u> of <u>Lady Macbeth</u> and <u>Macbeth</u>. Refer to this extract from Act 1 Scene 5 and <u>elsewhere</u> in the play.

OR

<u>How and why</u> do you think <u>Macbeth's relationship with Banquo</u> changes? Explore at least <u>two</u> moments from the play to support your ideas.

NB for OCR the alternative essay question will not be related to the extract.

Eduqas

(a) What does this extract <u>show an audience</u> about <u>Lady Macbeth's character</u> and her <u>relationship</u> with her husband at this point in the play? Refer <u>closely</u> to <u>details</u> from the extract to support your answer.

*(b) Write about <u>how</u> Shakespeare presents the <u>relationship between Macbeth and Banquo</u> at <u>different points</u> in the play.

*5 marks are allocated to this question for accuracy in spelling, punctuation and the use of grammar.

NB for Eduqas the second question will not be related to the extract.

Spot the differences

- Only OCR gives you a choice of an extract-based question *or* an essay unrelated to the extract.

- AQA and OCR do not divide the answer into sections and refer to the **whole play**.

- Edexcel and Eduqas divide the answer into two parts, with part (a) requiring close discussion of the extract. Edexcel awards marks for AO2 only in part (a) of the question.

- Edexcel part (b) will require you to write about a linked theme, uses the phrase **elsewhere in the play** and awards marks to AO1 and AO3.

- Eduqas only asks for discussion on the extract. The second part of the question – on an unrelated topic – will ask you to discuss the whole play.

- Eduquas does not test AO3 in this question.

- Edexcel does not give marks to AO4 in this question.

'Working' the text

- If you are answering all or part of a task based on an extract, your next step is to *read the passage* very carefully, trying to get an overview or general impression of what is going on, and what or who is being described.

- Then *read* the extract again, underlining or highlighting any words or short phrases that you think might be related to the focus of the question and are of special interest. For example, they might be surprising, unusual or shocking in some way. You might have a strong emotional or analytical reaction to them or you might think that they are particularly clever or noteworthy.

- To gain high marks for an AO2 response, you have to consider how words and phrases may work together to produce a particular effect or to get you to think about a particular theme, and you have to explore the methods the writer uses to present a character in a particular way for their own purposes.

- You may pick out examples of literary techniques such as lists or use of imagery, or sound effects such as alliteration or onomatopoeia. You may spot an unusual word order, sentence construction or use of rhythm and rhyme.

GRADE *BOOSTER*

When you start writing you must try to explain the effects created by particular words/phrases or techniques, and not simply identify what they mean. AO2, the assessment objective concerned with language, is worth a high proportion of the marks, so your answer will have to demonstrate your understanding of how Shakespeare's imagery, diction, rhyme and so on help to communicate the character's thoughts to the audience.

Planning your answer

It is advisable to make a brief plan before you start writing your response to avoid repeating yourself or getting into a muddle. A plan is not a first draft. You will not have time to do this. In fact, if your plan consists of full sentences at all, you are probably eating into the time you have available for writing a really insightful and considered answer. A plan is important because it helps you to gather and organise your thoughts, but it should consist of brief words and phrases.

GRADE *BOOSTER*

Examiners recognise that a plan is often a sign that a response will be good. Planning really can help to raise your grade.

You may find it helpful to use a diagram of some sort – perhaps a **spider diagram** or **flow chart**. This may help you to keep your mind open to new ideas as you plan, so that you can slot them in. You could make a list instead. The important thing is to choose a method that works for you.

If you have made a spider diagram, arranging your thoughts is a simple matter of numbering the branches in the best possible order.

Writing your answer

You are ready to start writing your answer. Remember you are working against the clock so it is really important to use your time wisely.

You may not have time to deal with all of the points you wish to make in your response. If you simply identify several language features and make a brief comment on each, you will be working at a fairly low level. The idea is to **select** the features that you find most interesting and develop your comments in a sustained and detailed manner. In order to move up the grades in the mark scheme, it is important to write a lot about a little, rather than a little about a lot.

You must also remember to address the whole question as you will be penalised if you fail to do so. For example, if the question asks you to consider character and relationship you must refer to both of them in your answer.

If you have any time left at the end of the examination, do not waste it. Check carefully that your meaning is clear and that you have done the very best that you can. Look back at your plan and check that you have included all your best points. Is there anything else you can add? Keep thinking until you are told to put your pen down.

Referring to the author and title

You can refer to Shakespeare either by name (make sure you spell it correctly) or as 'the writer'. You should never use his first name (William – or, even worse, Bill) – this sounds as if you know him personally.

GRADE BOOSTER

Do not lose sight of the playwright in your essay. Remember that the play is a construct - the characters, their words, their actions and reactions, have all been created by Shakespeare - so most of your points need to be about what Shakespeare might have been trying to achieve. In explaining how his message is conveyed to you, for instance, through an event, an aspect of a character, use of symbolism, personification, irony and so on, do not forget to mention him.

For example:

- Shakespeare presents the audience with the information that….

- It is evident from…that Shakespeare is inviting the audience to consider….

- Here, the audience may well feel that the writer is suggesting….

Writing in an appropriate style

Remember that you are expected to write in a suitable **register**. This means that you need to use an *appropriate* style. You should:

- not use colloquial language or slang (except when quoting dialogue): 'Malcolm is a right wimp, so pathetic at fighting that he nearly gets captured.'

- not become too personal or anecdotal: 'Lady Macbeth reminds me of my English teacher, who can be really evil at times, but also very good with words and persuasion.'

- use suitable phrases for an academic essay. It is better to say 'It could be argued that…' rather than 'I reckon that…', or 'Banquo's words give the reader the impression that…' rather than 'This quote shows that….'
- not be too dogmatic. Do not say 'This means that….' It is much better to say 'This might suggest that….'

You are also expected to be able to use a range of technical terms correctly. The *Language, style and analysis* section of this guide should help with that. However, if you cannot remember the correct name for a technique but can still describe its effect, you should still go ahead and do so.

The first person ('I')

It is perfectly appropriate to say 'I feel' or 'I think'. You are being asked for your opinion. Just remember that you are being asked for your opinion about *what* Shakespeare may have been trying to convey in his play (his themes and ideas) and *how* he does this (through characters, events, language, form and structure of the play).

Spelling, punctuation and grammar (AO4)

Most exam boards specifically target **spelling, punctuation and grammar** (SPaG) (AO4) for assessment in the Shakespeare question, except for Edexcel. The marks available may not be as high as for the other objectives, but you cannot afford to forget that you will demonstrate your grasp of the play through the way you write, so take great care with this. You will throw away marks if you make careless errors. Even worse, if the examiner cannot understand what you are trying to say, they will not be able to give you credit for your ideas, so accuracy matters.

How to raise your grade

- Answer the question which is in front of you. You have only a short time in this exam, so get started as soon as you have gathered your thoughts together and made a brief plan.
- Sometimes students go into panic mode because they do not know how to start. It is absolutely fine to begin an extract-based response with the words, 'In this extract Shakespeare presents….'
- Pick out interesting words and phrases, and unpick or explore them within the context or focus of the question. For example, if the question is about the way that power is presented, you need to focus on words and phrases to do with power.
  - What methods has the playwright used? It might be something as simple as a powerful adjective. What impact do you think this has? It might be that the word you are referring to has more than one meaning. If so, the examiner will be impressed if you can discuss what the word means to you, but can also suggest other meanings.

- Is context relevant? For instance, would Shakespeare's readers view power differently? What might Shakespeare have been trying to express about power when he chose this word or phrase?

- It is likely that you will find it easier to address AO2 (methods) when writing about the extract as you have the actual words in front of you. Is there an overall effect? For instance, you may have noticed Shakespeare's frequent use of images of blood and milk which create intensely vivid impressions, so as well as analysing individual words, you could also describe the overall symbolic effect.

- Be careful about lapsing into narrative, or writing about a character as if he or she is a real person. For example, if you are asked about how Shakespeare presents Banquo, remember that the focus of the question is about the methods that Shakespeare uses. Do not simply tell the examiner what Banquo does or what he is like – this is a very common mistake.

- Remember most exam boards also ask you to deal with an aspect of the question related to the rest of the play, not just the extract. If you feel you have more to offer in terms of comments on the extract, leave a space so that you can return to it if you have time.

Key points to remember

- Do not just jump straight in – time spent wisely in those first moments may gain you extra marks later.

- Write a brief plan.

- Remember to answer the question.

- Refer closely to *details* in the passage in your answer, support your comments and, where asked, remember that you must also refer to the play as a whole or refer to 'elsewhere' in the play.

- Use your time wisely. Try to leave a few minutes to look back over your work and check your spelling, punctuation and grammar, so that your meaning is clear and so that you know you have done the very best that you can.

- Keep an eye on the clock.

You need to make original points clearly and succinctly and convince the examiner that your viewpoint is really your own, and a valid one, with constant and careful reference to the text. This will be aided by the use of short and apposite (meaning really relevant) quotations, skilfully embedded in your answer along the way.

GRADE **BOOSTER**

Beware! Extract questions might look easy but they require you to show knowledge of other parts of the play as well as the printed extract, so make sure you write a full answer to the question.

GRADE **BOOSTER**

Less successful answers often consist of a series of supported points, where explanations of evidence fail to probe deeply. Try to vary how you present evidence and work at your explanations. Show your ability to analyse ideas *and* features of style. Offer alternative interpretations where you can. This will help you to reach grade 8 or 9.

GRADE FOCUS

Grade 5

Students will have a clear focus on the text and the task and will be able to 'read between the lines'. They will develop a clear understanding of the ways in which writers use language, form and structure to create effects for the readers. They will use a range of detailed textual evidence to support comments. They will show understanding of the idea that both writers and readers may be influenced by where, when and why a text is produced.

Grade 8

Students will produce a consistently convincing, informed response to a range of meanings and ideas within the text. They will use ideas which are well-linked and will often build on one another. They will dig deep into the text, examining, exploring and evaluating the writer's use of language, form and structure. They will carefully select finely judged textual references which are well integrated in order to support and develop their response to the text. They will show perceptive understanding of how contexts shape texts and responses to texts.

Aiming for a Grade 9

To reach the very highest level you need to have thought about the play more deeply and produce a response which is conceptualised, critical and exploratory at a deeper level. You might, for instance, challenge accepted critical views in evaluating whether the writer has always been successful. If, for example, you think Shakespeare set out to create increased respect for the monarchy of his time, how successful do you think he has been?

You may feel that the creation of respect for the monarchy veers into propaganda for King James I at times: it might be described as manipulation of the contemporary audience through fear, though this may be an aspect of the play lost on a secular modern audience. Does the presentation of the witches, Banquo's ghost and the ultimate fate of Macbeth lack credibility, or seem overly sensational? Do you consider this a problem for a modern audience or not?

REVIEW YOUR LEARNING

1 On which paper is your *Macbeth* question?
2 Can you take your copy of the play into the exam?
3 Will you have a choice of question?
4 How long do you have to answer the question?
5 What advice would you give to another student about using quotations?
6 Will you be assessed on spelling, punctuation and grammar in your response to *Macbeth*?
7 Why is it important to plan your answer?
8 What should you do if you finish ahead of time?
Answers on p. 112.

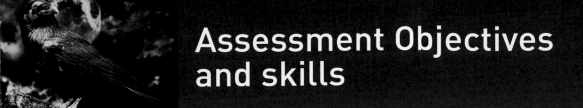

Assessment Objectives and skills

All GCSE examinations are pinned to specific areas of learning that the examiners want to be sure the candidates have mastered. These are known as Assessment Objectives or AOs. The same Assessment Objectives apply to your response to *Macbeth* whether you are studying it as an examination text for AQA, Eduqas, OCR or Edexcel. The examiner marking your response will be using the particular mark scheme for that board, but all mark schemes are based on fulfilling the key AOs for English Literature.

Assessment Objectives

What skills do you need to show?

Let's break down the Assessment Objectives to analyse what they really mean.

> **AO1** Read, understand and respond to texts. Students should be able to:
> - Maintain a critical style and develop an informed personal response.
> - Use textual references, including quotations, to support and illustrate interpretations.

At its most basic level, this AO is about having a good grasp of what a text is about, and being able to express an opinion about it within the context of the question. For example, if you were to say, 'The play is about an ambitious warrior called Macbeth' you would be beginning to address AO1 because you have made a personal response. An **informed** response refers to the basis on which you make that judgement. In other words, you need to show that you know the play well enough to answer the question.

Closely linked to this is the idea that you are also required to **use textual references, including quotations, to support and illustrate interpretations.** This means giving short direct quotations from the text. For example, if you wanted to support the idea that Macbeth could be fierce in battle, you could use a direct quote to point to his skill with a sword: 'his brandished steel...smoked with bloody execution'. Alternatively, you could simply refer to details in the text, in order to support your views. So you might say, 'Macbeth is shown to be a fierce warrior by the Captain's description of how he takes on the Norwegian army and claims many enemy lives.'

Generally speaking, most candidates find AO1 relatively easy. Usually, it is tackled well – if you answer the question you are asked, this Assessment Objective will probably take care of itself.

> **AO2** Analyse the language, form and structure used by a writer to create meanings and effects, using relevant subject terminology where appropriate.

AO2 is not as easy as AO1. Most examiners would probably agree that covering AO2 is a weakness for many candidates, particularly those students who only ever talk about the characters as if they are real people.

In simple terms, AO2 refers to the writer's methods and is often signposted in questions by the word 'how' or the phrase 'how does the writer present....'

Overall AO2 is easily overlooked, so it is vital that you are fully aware of this objective. The word **language** refers to Shakespeare's use of words, imagery or style. Remember that writers choose words very carefully in order to achieve particular effects. They may spend a long time deciding between two or three words which are similar in meaning in order to create the precise effect that they are looking for.

If you are addressing AO2 in your response to *Macbeth*, you will typically find yourself using Shakespeare's name and exploring the choices he has made. For example, Lady Macbeth's speech to the spirits (1.5 36–52) includes references to milk and breasts, which Shakespeare employs to symbolise nurture and compassion, but also to blood, which symbolises destruction, death and evil. Language choice here is communicating an abstract idea which links with the play's themes. It is this explanation that addresses AO2, whereas 'Lady Macbeth asks the spirits to take away her femininity' is a simple AO1 comment.

Language also encompasses a wide range of the writer's methods, such as the choice of diction, use of verse form, words which create sound effects, irony and so on.

AO2 also refers to your use of **subject terminology**. This means that you should be able to use terms such as *metaphor*, *alliteration* and *hyperbole* with confidence and understanding. However, if you cannot remember the term, do not despair – you will still gain marks for explaining the effects being created.

The terms **form** and **structure** refer to the kind of text you are studying and how it has been 'put together' by the writer. This might include the narrative technique being used, which would include dramatic devices like the soliloquy, the genre(s) the text is part of, the order of events and the effects created by it. In *Macbeth*, for example, Shakespeare follows the narrative structure of a classical tragedy, as Scotland descends from order to chaos. The way key events are juxtaposed may also be significant, for example, the comic relief scene involving the Porter which comes between the highly dramatic scenes where Duncan is murdered and his body is discovered by Macduff.

Remember – if you do not address AO2 at all, it will be very difficult to achieve much higher than Grade 1, since you will not be answering the question.

> **AO3** Show understanding of the relationship between texts and the contexts in which they were written.

This AO, although perhaps not as important as AO1 and AO2, is still worth between 15% and 20% of your total mark in the examination as a whole, and so should not be underestimated. You need to check your exam board to see what proportion of the AO3 marks are given to the question on *Macbeth*.

To cover AO3 you must show that you understand the links between a text and when, why and for whom it was written. For example, you might show some awareness of how a seventeenth-century audience would have a shared understanding of Christian beliefs and social hierarchy, and understand that this aspect of the play is less clear to audiences today.

You might also consider literary context: for example, Greek classical tragedy, or the ideas that Shakespeare used and those he changed from the original tale by Holinshed. Some understanding of the theatre in London in Shakespeare's time might be relevant. For example, the lack of lighting effects at the time meant that there was a practical need to refer to darkness or light at certain points in the play. Knowing that Shakespeare was also an actor and a keen theatre-goer could also be relevant.

However, it is important to understand that context should not be 'bolted on' to your response for no good reason – you are writing about literature, not history.

> **AO4** Use a range of vocabulary and sentence structures for clarity, purpose and effect, with accurate spelling and punctuation.

This AO is fairly self-explanatory and it is worth remembering that it is likely to be assessed in some part of your response to *Macbeth*, unless your exam board is Edexcel. Well-constructed sentences, accurate punctuation and well-chosen, accurately spelled vocabulary is as important as it is in your English Language exam.

A clear and well-written response should always be your aim, even where no marks are given to this AO. If your spelling is so bad or your grammar and lack of punctuation so confusing that the examiner cannot understand what you are trying to express, this will obviously adversely affect your mark.

Similarly, although there are no marks awarded for good handwriting, and none taken away for untidiness or crossings out, it is important that the examiner can read what you have written. If you believe your handwriting is so illegible that it may cause difficulties for the examiner, you need to speak to your school's examination officer in plenty of time before the exam. They may be able to arrange for you to have a scribe or to sit your examination using a computer.

Common mistakes

- **Retelling the story.** A key feature of the lowest grades is 'retelling the story'. Do not do this.

- **Quoting long passages.** Remember, every reference and piece of quotation must serve a specific point you are making. If you quote at length, the examiner will have to guess which bit of the quotation you mean to serve your point. Be explicit about exactly which words you have found specific meaning in. Keep quotations short and smart.

- **Merely identifying literary devices.** You will never gain marks simply for identifying literary devices such as a simile or metaphor. Similarly, you will gain no marks for pointing out that 'Shakespeare uses iambic pentameters in this speech.' However, you can gain marks by offering a thoughtful consideration of how literary devices might impact on readers, as well as an evaluation of how effective you think they are.

- **Giving unsubstantiated opinions.** The examiner will be keen to give you marks for your opinions, but only if they are supported by reasoned argument and references to the text. Therefore, you will get no marks for writing 'Everyone thinks that Macbeth is a total baddie, but I don't.' You *will* get marks for 'It is easy to show that Shakespeare presents Macbeth as a brutal tyrant and ruthless murderer. However, evidence from the end of the play redeems him somewhat as we see him put on his armour and fight bravely to the end.'

- **Writing about characters as if they are real people.** It is important to remember that characters are constructs – the writer is responsible for what the characters do and say.

REVIEW YOUR LEARNING

1 How many Assessment Objectives (AOs) are there?

2 What does AO1 assess?

3 What sort of material do you need to cover to address AO2 successfully?

4 What aspects of the text should you write about to gain AO3 marks?

5 What aspects of your writing does AO4 cover? Is it assessed in your *Macbeth* answer?

6 Which exam board specification are you following and what AOs should you be focusing on?

7 What should you **not** do in your responses?

Answers on p. 112.

Sample essays

Target your thinking

- What features does a grade 5 essay have?
- How does a grade 8 essay improve on that?
- What makes for a good introduction and conclusion?
- What is an 'appropriate' essay style?

Sample responses to two exam questions are provided below. The responses are from two students working at different levels. You should be able to see how Student Y takes similar material to that of Student X, but develops it further in order to achieve a higher grade.

AQA-style question and response

The question below is typical of an AQA question which requires you to consider both an extract and the play as a whole.

Read the following extract from Act 1 scene 5 of *Macbeth* and then answer the question that follows.

LADY MACBETH

...Come, you spirits
That tend on mortal thoughts, unsex me here,
And fill me from the crown to the toe top-full
Of direst cruelty! Make thick my blood;
Stop up the access and passage to remorse,
That no compunctious visitings of nature
Shake my fell purpose, nor keep peace between
The effect and it! Come to my woman's breasts,
And take my milk for gall, you murdering ministers,
Wherever in your sightless substances
You wait on nature's mischief! Come, thick night,
And pall thee in the dunnest smoke of hell,
That my keen knife see not the wound it makes,
Nor heaven peep through the blanket of the dark,
To cry 'Hold, hold!'

Starting with this extract, explain how far you think that Shakespeare presents Lady Macbeth as a strong and influential character. Write about:

- how Shakespeare presents Lady Macbeth in this speech
- how Shakespeare presents Lady Macbeth in the play as a whole   [30 marks]

AO4 [4 marks]

In addressing the first bullet, both students looked at the extract and began by considering how Lady Macbeth's character and appearance are presented. Student X, who is likely to achieve grade 5, began the response like this:

> I am going to write about Lady Macbeth and will decide if she is strong and influential in this speech and in the rest of the play. This is the first time Lady Macbeth appears on stage and she makes a big impression on the audience because she comes across as determined, visious and evil. When Lady Macbeth makes speeches Shakespeare writes in blank verse to make them dramatic. Straight away she begins to think about murdering the king as she speaks this soliloquy of her true thoughts to the audience.

1 There are no marks for this kind of introduction. At this point the examiner may well be thinking, 'Well get on with it, then.'

2 Focus is on the extract and awareness shown of the play as a whole.

3 Attempt to comment on features of style – could be more developed (AO2).

4 Some understanding of dramatic devices but no real AO2 analysis as yet.

Student Y, who is likely to achieve grade 8, began the response like this:

> In this important speech, Shakespeare provides the audience with evidence which reveals aspects of the character of Lady Macbeth in several ways, one of which is to link her with the evil of the weird sisters as she invites the powers of evil into her body and her soul. 'Spirits that tend on mortal thoughts' and 'murdering ministers' both reference the witches and the alliterative 'm' sound emphasises the words which denote their evil intent, emphasising the extent to which the death of Duncan is what is on her mind, but also to remind the audience that these forces ('ministers') are intimately linked with the 'mischief' loving weird sisters. The word 'mortal' is ambiguous as it could mean a living being – human thoughts - or it could mean thoughts about death. Both meanings are relevant here.

1 Strong introduction – refers to both aspects of the question, making an important thematic connection between Lady Macbeth and the supernatural.

2 Immediate focus on a language device with well-integrated textual detail and sophisticated analysis (AO2).

Both students then continued by looking in detail at how Lady Macbeth invokes the devil to make her stronger.

Student X wrote:

> She begins by saying:
>
> 'Come, you spirits
>
> That tend on mortal thoughts', unsex me here!'
>
> Shakespeare shows her asking evil forces to stop her from being a woman, that is what 'unsex' means. She says she wants to be filled right up with 'direst cruelty' which makes it sound as if she believes that women are not naturally like that, but usually kind and loving instead, which was the stereotype of women even more in the 1600s than now., Although she is strong and makes quick decisions maybe she needs extra strength from outside to be able to influence her husband.
>
> She carries on asking the spirits to make her blood thick. Blood is a word that Shakespeare repeats all the way through Macbeth and it is always associated with death and killing, which is what is on Lady Macbeth's mind here, which shows her strength. On the other hand she then says a perculiar thing when she asks them to take her breasts away, and she talks about 'milk for gall' This means she couldn't feed a baby, which is what a natural woman would do. Things that are unnatural are an important theme in Macbeth. She is part of that theme, acting more dominant and much more harsh than women in those times were expected to be.

1 Well-chosen quotation, though not linked with the later mention of spirits, so the point is not fully developed (AO1).

2 Clear point made about detail of language (AO2) and clear link to the task (AO1).

3 Reference to context (AO3).

4 Clear focus on topic of Lady Macbeth's strength (AO1).

5 Language detail identified clearly, but incomplete understanding – blood has further significance here as a life force (AO2).

6 Relevant quotation selected (AO1), but evidence of misreading – it is the milk that is to be taken, not the breasts (AO2).

7 A relevant point made here, and further reference to historical context (AO3).

Student Y wrote:

> She certainly is presented to us as an immensely strong and decisive woman: her soliloquy is powerful, imperative in tone, though maybe Shakespeare puts doubt into our minds as to whether Lady Macbeth is innately evil if she has to resort to this: commanding demons to 'unsex

1 Precise focus on question (AO1).

2 Context integrated into the answer.

5 Shows clear understanding of complex content – very sophisticated level of analysis (A01/A03).

> her' and later to possess the most feminine part of her, her breasts, and to turn her milk to bitter 'gall'. These words imply that she has the qualities of a stereotypical woman of Jacobean times such as kindness, nurture, moral scruples, for why else would she need to ask for supernatural help to make her stong?
>
> Instead, she asks to be filled 'top-full/Of direst cruelty' and for her blood to become so thick that 'no compunctious visitings of nature/ Shake my fell purpose'. This implies that conscience flows around the body like blood, also demonstrating that Lady Macbeth is well aware that she is going against God and 'nature', in all she asks in this speech, another important thematic link between the supernatural and the chaos unleashed by 'supernatural soliciting' as Macbeth called it earlier.

3 Precise choice of short quotations with close analysis of their significance. Terminology integrated into comment (A02).

4 Sophisticated knowledge about historical context (A03) integrated with perceptive comment on complex language (A02).

6 Convincing links between themes (A01).

Both students then continued by examining the extended metaphor at the end of the speech.

Student X wrote:

2 Clear linking of theme and stylistic devices (A01 and A02).

> She asks the spirits again, this time she calls them 'murdering ministers', which is a good bit of alliteration to make these words stand out. When she talks about mischief, it reminds us of the witches. Shakespeare makes it sound as if she is selling her soul to the devil. Shakespeare ends up the speech with personification of light and darkness when she asks for the night to be as dark as 'the dunnest smoke of hell' which also links with the devil and sounds really dark and evil. In some ways she seems very strong here, if she is prepared to go to hell, but in other ways, if she has to ask for help to be able to behave in a way that goes against her femininity, maybe she isn't as strong as she thinks.

1 Correct terminology and brief comment on style (A02).

3 Clear focus on question and development of personal opinion (A01).

She wants it to be so dark that God in heaven can't see through 'the blanket of the dark' and even the knife she is thinking about using to kill the king won't be able to see what harm it's doing: 'see not the wound it makes'. This is Lady Macbeth's big mistake, as it turns out, because hiding evil doesn't make it go away.

4 Clear analysis of a complex sequence of images here, well supported with quoted detail (AO1 and AO2).

5 Final comment leads neatly into the second part of the question (AO1).

Student Y wrote:

With contrasting disturbing and unnatural images of thickened blood and bitter milk Shakespeare moves the audience into even more explicitly evil territory as a string of personification concludes the speech, almost as if to show Lady Macbeth shifting any blame to objects around her. The mention of 'sightless substances' develops into an invocation of the dark of night to descend:

'And pall thee in the dunnest smoke of hell'

that is, that the normal darkness will be covered by a 'shroud' (further associations with death) of utter blackness from hell, thus blinding the knife she must be imagining using on Duncan, and further, acting as a 'blanket' so that the forces of good, or God in heaven, will not see the terrible sin she is planning.

Shakespeare seems to be showing that she is delusional, for any Christian at that time would believe that God sees everything, however Lady Macbeth is presented as thinking that what appears to be the case is the same as reality (another theme) so if she does not name the deed and conceals the act and its consequences, it will not have happened.

1 Sophisticated and detailed analysis of imagery convincingly linked together (AO2).

2 Detailed and sophisticated analysis of a complex image (AO2).

3 Exploration of context integrated with detailed grasp of themes (AO3).

The students then moved on to respond to the second bullet point – how Lady Macbeth's character is developed in 'the play as a whole'.

Student X wrote:

1 Clear focus on question (A01).

2 Reference to relevant detail (A01).

3 Clear summary of several relevant events to support personal opinion (A01).

4 Well-chosen quoted evidence (A01). Clear reference to language detail (A02).

5 Clear response to the task (A01).

6 Clear conclusion – focus on task (A01). Also implicit grasp of context.

Later in the play Shakespeare shows us how Lady Macbeth goes mad with guilt at what she has done, so maybe she wasn't really as tough as she seemed. When she and Macbeth murdered Duncan she set the murder up but she admits she couldn't do it herself as he reminded her of her 'father as he slept'. She does take the daggers back to the murder scene, which is a powerful act, and she makes sure that Macbeth doesn't give them away when the body is discovered by Macduff. At times she is very strong and influential. She does the same thing, showing power and influence to the whole court when he sees Banquo's ghost, though once they are on their own, she seems quite vulnerable when he won't discuss anything with her.

By the end of the play she is insane, and her female guilt and weakness all comes out when she is sleep-walking. She keeps rubbing her hands together and talking about a spot of blood:

'Out, damned spot! Out I say.'

In her mind, she remembers little details of the night Macbeth killed Duncan, like how she told him to wash his hands to cover up the murder, but now she can't get her hands clean at all.

She says: 'who would have thought the old man to have so much blood in him,' which must be remembering how she took the daggers back into the room and shows her guilt and feminine weakness.

The theme of light and darkness is in this speech too when she says: 'Hell is murky.' She must be frightened of going to hell now. She wanted it to be dark to cover up their crimes but now she has a light by her bed all the time. She must be scared of the devil and what she has done. When she needed to be strong for her husband, she could act in a very powerful and influential way, but in the end she can't stop being a woman.

Student X has written a grade 5 answer. The key word is CLEAR. It focuses on the task set and makes relevant comment on features of Shakespeare's language and on thematic links. As an answer, it generally manages to avoid storytelling and selects relevant evidence from the text to support the points. Spelling is occasionally careless and expression a little informal at times.

Student Y wrote in much more detail and continued to focus on aspects of language:

1 Exploration of context integrated with insightful comment on religious beliefs (AO3).

Lady Macbeth is presented as at her most powerful and controlling when she talks her conscience-stricken husband into committing the treacherous and sinful act of assassinating the King, at that time seen as being analogous with killing God himself. She manipulates his warrior, male pride by repeatedly calling him a coward. At this point in the play she is very obviously the stronger of the two.

When the couple perform the murder of Duncan, she is strong for her husband, though alone she is shown to be jumpy, admitting she has been drinking for courage. Her femininity still influences her as she confesses that she was unable to kill Duncan herself as he 'looked like my father as he slept'.

2 Adept summary of subsequent events with deft integration of supporting detail (AO1).

However for Macbeth she is ever powerful: encouraging him to wash his hands and cover up his guilt by putting on a night gown and pretending they are newly awake when Macduff and company arrive for the King. Similarly she fends off discovery by decisively taking control of events when Macbeth almost gives himself away with bizarre behaviour at their banquet. Although he has told her nothing of his murderous plans for Banquo ('be innocent of the knowledge...'), her words make it clear that she suspects what has happened. Increasingly, as Macbeth tries to secure his position as King alone, she has no role to play in terms of power or influence. She is not seen on stage again until the end of the play.

3 Focus still firmly on the task supported by excellent textual knowledge (AO1).

Her final appearance is in stark contrast with the strong woman she was trying to be. Guilt drives her insane, her disordered mind reflected in Shakespeare's use of prose, rather than the powerful blank verse of her opening soliloquy. She begins sleep-walking, also somewhat ironic as Macbeth was the one we heard say he had 'murder[ed] sleep' after Duncan's death. Guilt in her conscience is symbolised by the spot of blood she cannot remove from her hands. It is a 'damned spot' so in this scene Shakespeare reminds us of her pact with the forces of evil, though now she is not so welcoming of the darkness of hell, describing it fearfully as 'murky'. Her gentle-woman tells the doctor 'she has light by her constantly' which symbolises her fear of the dark and of evil in general.

Her thoughts shift around Macbeth's various victims, but constantly return to the night of Duncan's death when she instructed Macbeth: 'Wash your hands', to remove the evidence of their crime. Now she knows that appearing to be innocent is not the reality, as she rubs her hands together and laments that:

'...all the perfumes of Arabia will not sweeten this little hand.'

Though she had no responsibility for the deaths of Banquo or Lady Macduff, she speaks about having their blood on her hands, or rather on her conscience judging from her final speech.

Lady Macbeth shows us the consequences of evil. She dies shortly afterwards and the end of the play gives hints that her death was suicide. She began as Macbeth's 'partner in greatness' and ends in this pitiful state, neither strong nor influential. In the end her femininity could not be taken away.

4 Conceptualised answer – perceptive links made between different parts of the text (AO1).

5 Focus on details of language – comment shows insight (AO2).

6 Thematic linking of contrasting details from this scene and Act 2 (AO1).

91

This is a good grade 8 answer, combining a discussion of how Lady Macbeth's character is presented and her relationship with her husband. There is sophisticated analysis of Shakespeare's use of language – skilfully drawing out parallels and contrasts between the scenes discussed. The answer focuses on the task and is logically argued. Textual evidence supports all points made. It contains a high quality analysis and evaluation of language features, with confident use of literary technical vocabulary. Specific and integrated comment is made on social and historical context and the answer is consistently accurate and fluently expressed (AO4).

Edexcel-style question and response

The question below is typical of an Edexcel question. These questions have two separate parts. The first part is extract based and may involve exploring character, relationships or feelings. The second part identifies a theme or idea in the extract and asks how this is presented elsewhere in the play.

You should spend about 55 minutes on this section.

You should divide your time equally between parts (a) and (b) of the question.

Macbeth – from act 1 scene 6, lines 11 to 32

Enter LADY MACBETH

DUNCAN

See, see, our honour'd hostess!
The love that follows us sometime is our trouble,
Which still we thank as love. Herein I teach you
How you shall bid God yield us for your pains,
And thank us for your trouble.

LADY MACBETH

                    All our service
In every point twice done and then done double
Were poor and single business to contend
Against those honours deep and broad wherewith
Your majesty loads our house: for those of old,
And the late dignities heap'd up to them,
We rest your hermits.

DUNCAN

          Where's the thane of Cawdor?
We coursed him at the heels, and had a purpose
To be his purveyor: but he rides well;
And his great love, sharp as his spur, hath holp him
To his home before us. Fair and noble hostess,
We are your guest to-night.

LADY MACBETH

           Your servants ever
Have theirs, themselves and what is theirs, in compt,
To make their audit at your highness' pleasure,
Still to return your own.

DUNCAN

         Give me your hand;
Conduct me to mine host: we love him highly,
And shall continue our graces towards him.
By your leave, hostess.

In this extract, Lady Macbeth welcomes Duncan to Macbeth's castle immediately after they have agreed a plan to murder him.

(a) Explore how Shakespeare presents the contrasting characters of Duncan and Lady Macbeth in this extract.

Refer closely to the extract in your answer.

(b) In this extract, Lady Macbeth deceives King Duncan.

Explain the importance of deception and manipulation elsewhere in the play.

In your answer you must consider:

- when others are deceived and/or manipulated
- the reasons why they are deceived

You should refer to the context of the play in your answer.

Part (a)

Student X, who is likely to achieve grade 5, answered part (a) as follows:

1 Clear focus on task.

> In this extract Shakespeare presents a massive contrast between the good King Duncan and the evil Lady Macbeth. The scene is full of irony as we see Duncan thanking Lady Macbeth for the 'love' she shows and 'trouble' she has taken to

prepare for his visit. He even calls her 'honoured hostess' and 'fair and noble hostess' but the audience knows that she has just persuaded her husband to murder Duncan while he is staying. Duncan repeats the word 'love' but what she feels for him is the opposite.

2 Selection of relevant words and phrases and clear AO2 commentary.

They both speak in blank verse because they are characters with high status and this is a formal and polite conversation. For Duncan it is genuine – he says all sorts of polite things and praises Macbeth when he says 'he rides well' and 'we love him highly'. What Lady Macbeth says is totally dishonest. She says what they have done to make him welcome is 'poor and single business' and even if they had done twice as much it wouldn't be enough to thank him for what he has done to honour them.

3 Recognition of purpose of blank verse. Clear AO2 point.

4 Less successful on Shakespeare's use of blank verse to present Lady Macbeth's character but focus still on relevant aspects of meaning of selected phrases.

It is very exaggerated as well as ironic because she is thanking Duncan for making Macbeth the Thane of Cawdor when she says about 'late dignities'. But what she is really doing is preparing to get rid of Duncan so Macbeth can be king. The way some of the blank verse lines are shared during this conversation like 'We are your guest tonight/Your servants ever' also gives the impression that she finds it easy to say these lying words.

5 Appropriate use of critical terminology – clear AO2.

6 Appropriate use of critical terminology – clear AO2.

Duncan is too good to think anything bad of them. There is a simile when he talks about how fast Macbeth rode home, 'sharp as his spur' because he loves Lady Macbeth so much. This is ironic too because he rode home so fast to speak to her about what the witches said and to tell her Duncan was coming. The way Shakespeare wrote this scene really contrasts Duncan's godly character with lying scheming Lady Macbeth.

7 Some grasp of a more sophisticated technique.

8 Retains a focus on the task and on AO2.

Student Y, who is likely to achieve grade 8, answered part (a) as follows:

1 Insight about task and the AO2 focus of it.

Here we see Shakespeare using a range of language devices to develop one of the major themes of the play, that is how deceptive appearance can be. The characters of King Duncan and Lady Macbeth are presented as contrasting facets of this theme. Duncan is presented as so trusting as to be gullible, while Shakespeare shows us how Lady Macbeth is devious and scheming, beneath her 'innocent flower' like appearance. She has clearly taken her earlier advice to her husband to heart. The scene is thus heavily ironic. First we see Duncan greeting her as 'honoured hostess' and later 'fair and noble hostess'. This reminds us of his propensity to be taken in by appearance – he earlier commented that he had trusted the traitor Thane of Cawdor, but been deceived by him. It is deeply ironic that the very man who now has that title as a reward given to him by Duncan has just been persuaded to kill him, by the woman he now greets.

Duncan's use of the royal 'we' reminds us of his regal status, while his diction reflects his goodness almost apologising that the 'love' his subjects feel for him causes them to go to excessive 'trouble'. He thanks her profusely saying that God will reward her, reminding us of the sanctity of his role, and later says he will 'continue [his] graces towards [Macbeth]' – another word with religious resonance - little knowing that the 'trouble' they are taking is to plan his murder.

Both characters' dialogue is spoken in blank verse, reflecting the formal and courtly situation. Duncan's speech is sincere as he compliments both his hosts, mentioning his regard for Macbeth: 'he rides well' and 'we love him highly'. The simile he uses comparing Macbeth's love for her 'sharp as his spur' is also ironic in two ways

2 Precise reference to language devices elsewhere in the text to support this analysis.

3 Judicious use of subject terminology underpins well-developed and exploratory analysis supported by very well chosen textual reference – very strong AO2 here.

4 Perceptive AO2 analysis continues.

5 Sophisticated exploration of religious diction – links with theme and context.

– first because of the real motive he had for his speedy return – and also because it foreshadows the image he uses in the following scene where Lady Macbeth becomes the 'spur' to his ambition.

There is an interesting use of stichomythia as their speeches merge into each other: 'We are your guest tonight/Your servants ever'. In the main this technique builds tension in dialogue, but here it is almost the opposite, making their speech seem to flow seamlessly – which is another ironic feature since it could be underlining how easy Lady Macbeth finds it to manipulate others with deceitful words.

6 Very perceptive and developed commentary on verse form and its effects.

Part (b)

The next two sample responses are based on part (b), a question which often requires exploration of a theme.

Student X produced the following answer for part (b):

2 For Edexcel, there are no marks for AO2 in a part (b) question, but this will gain AO1 marks for showing understanding of the implicit meaning of the opening scene.

3 Though generally accurate in expression, 'con' is not appropriate formal language.

Deception and manipulation are part of the theme of appearance and reality. The witches start this theme right at the beginning of the play. The audience is confused when they speak in riddles and opposites, like 'when the battle's lost and won' and their words are not to be trusted. They make deceptive and manipulative promises to Macbeth and Banquo twice in the play. Their words come true, but not in the obvious way. At the start they more or less con Macbeth into believing them by telling him he will be Thane of Cawdor and then king. The audience has already seen Duncan reward him with Cawdor's title so when Macbeth is told of this, it is obvious that he will believe them, and he starts to imagine murdering Duncan straight away.

Lady Macbeth shows her own manipulation, when Shakespeare presents her persuading Macbeth to do the deed. She calls him a coward:

1 Clear opening sentence and theme is instantly identified – no time-wasting with this as an introduction.

4 Clear summary of opening scenes with relevant detail summarised (AO1).

'live a coward in thine own esteem'

and goes on to ask if he is really a proper man.

And she says he doesn't really love her if he won't go through with his promise to her:

'such I account thy love.'

This shows how good she is at using language to get her own way.

5 Detailed knowledge of the play and clear evidence that main ideas are understood (AO1).

She is very deceiving too. She really 'sucks up' to Duncan when he comes to stay and she gives Macbeth a lesson in deceiving when she says:

'Look like th'innocent flower,

But be the serpent under't.'

This is a simile which means you look all beautiful while you are actually really evil. Christians in the audience might see this as being about the devil in the Garden of Eden and Eve tempting Adam, as well.

6 Again, no marks for AO2 from Edexcel, however this evidence is closely linked to the theme and thus contributes to AO1 here. Comment about religion would gain some AO3 marks.

After the murder, she puts this into action when she takes back the bloody daggers, making it look like the king's servants did it, then she says 'a little water clears us of this deed and 'put on your nightgown' so it looks as if they have just got up and so no one will suspect they did anything. Shakespeare shows how she only partly deceives everyone though because Banquo and Macduff both show that they suspect something is going on.

7 Clear focus on task with relevant selection of detail both quoted and summarised (AO1).

8 Clear textual knowledge and commentary which shows engagement with implicit ideas (AO1).

After Macbeth has Banquo murdered he goes back to the witches to see what they have to promise him now. It is very like the first scene — they say three predictions about Macbeth, he must 'Beware Macduff', but they say he cannot be killed by 'man of woman born', which is a contradiction really. Then they tell him he will be king until 'Birnam Wood to Dunsinane hill do come....' Just like in the first promises, they have one for Banquo — they show Macbeth all of Banquo's ancestors in a long line with crowns, which is a symbol of how he will 'get kings' though he isn't one himself.

9 Clear summary and clear links between different parts of the play. (AO1 for Edexcel and could gain AO2 marks for grasp of structure from other boards).

At the end of the play Macbeth realises he has been tricked, when we see how the English army cut down trees for camouflage as they walk towards Dunsinane Castle, then Macduff says he was born by caesarean section and now we know how the witches deceived and manipulated Macbeth, so you can see how deception and manipulation are very important themes in Macbeth.

10 Task still clearly in focus, and a relevant concluding sentence (AO1).

Combining both sections, this is a grade 5 answer. The key word is CLEAR. It focuses on the task set and makes relevant comment on how the content of the text as a whole presents aspects of a central theme. It generally manages to avoid storytelling, and demonstrates an awareness of Shakespeare constructing the text. There is relevant evidence from the text to support the points. AO1 is stronger than AO3, but fewer marks are allocated to showing understanding of context so this weaker aspect would not lower the grade overall.

Student Y produced the following answer for part (b):

Deception is a key theme in 'Macbeth'. One of Lady Macbeth's most memorable lines, as she manipulates Macbeth into agreeing that they should murder Duncan so he can replace him as king is:

'Look like th'innocent flower,

But be the serpent under't.'

This simile shows exactly what we see so many times in the play: the outward show of goodness, the 'innocent flower' concealing the reality of deadly evil, the 'serpent' hiding beneath the flower, an image which reminds us of the devil in the form of a snake, corrupting Eve in the Garden of Eden. This is just one instance of Lady Macbeth's manipulative powers, where Shakespeare presents her using both words and actions skilfully to persuade her husband to do a deed that appals him.

1 Focus on task is clear from opening line – effective introduction (AO1).

3 Language detail immediately given as evidence – for Edexcel, there are no marks for AO2 in a part (b) question, but this will gain AO1 marks for convincing analysis of evidence which links the language of the play to symbolism of the central theme.

2 Contextual comment is perceptive (AO3).

At the outset of the play, Duncan commented that he had been deceived by the honest appearance of the Thane of Cawdor, who turned out to be a traitor:

'There's no art/To find the mind's construction in the face.'

This line also presents the audience with the concept of appearances being deceptive – and ironically the newly created Thane of Cawdor, Macbeth, deceives the king in all of their onstage interactions. 'Fairest show' (a phrase which reminds the audience of the witches) and a deceptive 'false face' conceal 'false heart' as the Macbeths plot to assassinate their guest. After the event, deceit is evident again as Shakespeare shows how they cover up their deed, making it look as if the king's servants did it; literally washing their hands of it; putting on their night clothes, so it seems they have just woken from sleep alongside the rest of the castle's occupants.

Both the Macbeths are presented as believing they can deceive God by covering their actions with darkness: she speaks of 'the dunnest smokes of hell' and he of 'seeling night', asking the personified darkness to 'Scarf up the tender eye of pitiful day.'

A contemporary Jacobean audience would have been well aware that God sees everything, and that the murder of his very representative on earth, or indeed any other terrible sin, would not be kept from the justice of the Almighty by deception. The final act of the play shows how their actions lead to their downfall as both Macbeth and Lady Macbeth die ignominiously.

The idea that appearance, how things seem, is not always the reality of the situation is presented over and over again in the play. The witches are the first clues to this, not

4 Conceptualised answer – judicious evidence from different parts of the text is woven into an informed response to the implicit as well as the explicit meaning.

5 More evidence of a conceptualised response with perceptive critical analysis of complex textual evidence (AO1).

6 Contextual detail woven into the argument (AO3) and closely related to the implicit meaning of main ideas and themes presented in the text (AO1).

7 Theme explained in an informed way with a sophisticated take on how it is presented in different aspects of the text (AO1).

so much their physical appearance (Banquo declares they look 'withered and...wild': strange, bearded women) but their words are constantly deceptive and manipulative. From the outset, they speak in a riddling way that Shakespeare labels as 'equivocation', and eventually Macbeth rails against 'the fiend/That lies like truth'. Their words show them to have a twisted take on reality: 'fair is foul and foul is fair', a difficult line to interpret, though maybe meaning that, to the witches, whatever we judge as good, they see as bad, conversely what we see as evil, to them is pleasing.

8 Once again, excellent choice of evidence which ranges around the whole text (AO1).

The second set of promises, given by the witches' 'masters', are even more equivocal: they seem to promise Macbeth ultimate safety – he can be killed by 'no man of woman born', and will reign in Scotland until a forest uproots itself and moves up a hill. When we are shown how these seeming impossibilities turn out to be completely possible – Macduff born by caesarean section and tree branches used to camouflage the English troops as they lay siege to Macbeth's castle, it is clear to the audience that the witches have deceived and manipulated Macbeth into doing their evil for them, just as much as Lady Macbeth's scolding and wheedling did in Act 1.

9 Perceptive and fluent analysis of significance of events with well-chosen integrated textual detail.

10 Informed linking of different parts of the text – perceptive on implicit meaning.

Ironically Banquo's words indicate that he saw through the witches at the start; 'The instruments of darkness.../Win us with honest trifles, to betray's....' Contemporary belief, informed in part by James I's fascination with witchcraft, was that witches could not cause death to humans by themselves – they had to find an agent to do this for them. Macbeth unleashes a storm of death before he ultimately dies himself, so they achieved great success here with their tempting 'honest trifles'.

11 Context woven into the argument in a way that strengthens the point being made (AO3 and AO1).

12 Convincing concluding sentence which shows a command of literary critical terms. ⟶

> *Deception and manipulation are, thus, key to the unfolding and resolution of the tragedy of Macbeth.*

Parts (a) and (b) combine to produce a good grade 8 answer, combining a discussion of this key theme with perceptive comment on aspects of the contemporary context of the play. Throughout there is evidence of a detailed knowledge of the whole text and of Shakespeare's skills as a writer. Evidence is apt and well integrated into the answer, skilfully drawing out parallels and contrasts between the scenes discussed.

Top ten

As your examination will be 'closed book' and you will only have a short extract in front of you, you might find it helpful to memorise some short quotations to use in support of your points in your examination response.

Top characterisation quotations

Macbeth

1 '...brave Macbeth (well he deserves that name)...' (1.2 16)
- The Captain's description reminds us that Macbeth begins the play as a triumphant warrior.

2 '...Thou wouldst be great,/Art not without ambition...' (1.5 17–18)
- Lady Macbeth identifies Macbeth's 'flaw'.

3 'This dead butcher...' (5.9 36)
- Malcolm's final word on Macbeth shows how far he has fallen.

Lady Macbeth

4 '...Come you spirits/That tend on mortal thoughts, unsex me here...' (1.5 38–39)
- Lady Macbeth asks the devil to take away her femininity so she will be strong enough to persuade Macbeth to kill Duncan, aligning her character with the weird sisters.

5 'Had he not resembled/My father as he slept, I had done't.' (2.2 12–13)
- Her reaction to the sleeping Duncan may indicate to the audience that she is still affected by feminine 'weakness'.

6 'All the perfumes of Arabia will not sweeten this little hand.' (5.1 42–43)
- By the end of the play, guilt has sent Lady Macbeth insane, perhaps indicating to us that it is impossible for a woman to escape her 'natural' femininity and her conscience.

Banquo

'Thou shalt get kings, though thou be none.' (1.3 65)

- The witches' promise to Banquo.

7

'Fly good Fleance!...' (3.3 20)

- Banquo's dying words, spoken in hope of saving his son from Macbeth's hired killers.

8

The weird sisters

'Fair is foul and foul is fair!' (1.1 12)

- The witches speak in riddles. For them, good is bad and bad is good, as they so clearly enjoy evil-doing.

9

Duncan

'Conduct me to mine host. We love him highly,/And shall continue our graces towards him.' (1.6 30–32)

- Duncan is presented as good personified, rewarding those who deserve it. Here he talks about Macbeth – and these words are called to mind during Macbeth's crisis of conscience at the end of Act 1.

10

Top moments in *Macbeth*

1 Third witch: 'All hail Macbeth, that shalt be King hereafter.' (1.3 48)

- These words set the plot in motion. Possibly the witches know that Macbeth, as an ambitious man, might have thought about becoming king.

2 Macbeth: 'My dearest love, Duncan comes here tonight.'
Lady Macbeth: 'And when goes hence?'
Macbeth: 'Tomorrow, as he purposes.'
Lady Macbeth: 'O! – Never Shall sun that morrow see!' (1.5 55–58)

- Lady Macbeth convinces her husband to seize the moment and kill Duncan when he arrives. Note the tension generated by the use of stichomythia, and the euphemistic way she speaks of Duncan's death.

3 'A little water clears us of this deed.' (2.2 70)

- Lady Macbeth reassures Macbeth when he loses control after Duncan's murder – shocked both by the blood on his hands and by knocking at the gate.

4 Donalbain: '... Where we are
There's daggers in men's smiles.' (2.3 132–133)

- When Duncan's sons make the decision to leave for places of safety, Donalbain's words foreshadow the violence that follows from Macbeth's reign of terror in Scotland.

5 'Thou hast it now - King, Cawdor, Glamis, all,
...and, I fear,
Thou playedst most foully for 't.' (3.1 1–3)

- Banquo's soliloquy speaks of his suspicion about Macbeth immediately he has been crowned king.

6 'Thou canst not say I did it! Never shake
Thy gory locks at me!' (3.4 50–51)

- Macbeth is tormented by Banquo's ghost during the banquet where his murdered friend was meant to be guest of honour.

'Beware Macduff!'
'...none of woman born/Shall harm Macbeth.' (4.1 70, 79–80)

7

- The witches continue to entice Macbeth to further violence – the contradiction of these promises is not lost on the audience.

'Seize upon Fife – give to the edge o' the sword/His wife, his babes, and all unfortunate souls/That trace him in his line.' (4.1 151–152)

8

- Macbeth orders the destruction of Macduff's entire household, having discovered Macduff is out of his reach in England.

'...Macduff was from his mother's womb/Untimely ripped.' (5.8 15–16)

9

- Macduff tells Macbeth that, instead of being 'born' in the normal way, he was delivered by caesarean section. The short line – four syllables instead of the usual ten – reflects Macbeth's shocked silence.

'Lay on, Macduff! –/And damned be him that first cries "Hold, enough!"' (5.8 33–34)

10

- Macbeth determines it better to die in battle than surrender to Malcolm. This final death leaves the way clear for Malcolm to become the rightful King of Scotland.

Top thematic quotations

Light and darkness

'signs of nobleness, like stars shall shine/On all deservers.' (1.4 41–42)

1

- Duncan promises to reward all who have served him in battle – the simile connects him with light and heaven.

'...Stars, hide your fires!/Let not light see my black and deep desires!'(1.4 50–51)

2

- Macbeth asks for darkness to conceal his evil thoughts and deeds.

'...Receive what cheer you may:/The night is long that never finds the day.' (4.3 242–243)

3

- Malcolm's rhyming couplet reminds us that light and goodness must be restored as the wheel of fortune turns, just as the light of day will follow night.

Order and chaos

4 Ross: '...Duncan's horses.../Turned wild in nature, broke their stalls/...as they would make/War with mankind.' (2.4 14–18)

- After Macbeth murders Duncan, nature 'turns wild' to reflect the cosmic chaos caused by the enormity of murdering God's chosen representative on Earth.

5 '...Each new morn,/New widows howl, new orphans cry.' (4.3 4–5)

- Macduff describes the effects of Macbeth's rule.

Appearance and reality

6 '...look like th'innocent flower/But be the serpent under't.' (1.5 63–64)

- Lady Macbeth's famous simile – the concept of looking harmless and attractive to conceal deadly intent recalls the serpent in Eden, the devil who tempted Eve, leading to the corruption of Adam.

7 '...mock the time with fairest show! –/False face must hide what the false heart doth know.' (1.7 81–82)

- Macbeth advises Lady Macbeth to carry on with the pretence of entertaining King Duncan as they plan his murder.

8 'Is this a dagger which I see before me...?' (2.1 33)

- Macbeth soliloquises about whether the dagger is real or merely an illusion.

The supernatural

9 'The instruments of darkness tell us truths;/Win us with honest trifles, to betray's/In deepest consequence.' (1.3 123–125)

- Banquo's prophetic words sum up the deception of Macbeth – the words of the witches tempt him with some truth – but they are not to be trusted.

10 'I...begin/To doubt th'equivocation of the fiend/That lies like truth.' (5.5 41–43)

- Macbeth's use of the word 'equivocation' shows he has realised that Banquo was right. The witches' words did not mean what they seemed to mean.

Wider reading

Plays

You might like to read or, even better, watch a production of another of Shakespeare's tragedies. *Hamlet*, *Othello* and *King Lear* share the central idea of the downfall of the tragic hero and include some similarities in their themes.

Graphic and modern English versions

Modern versions of *Macbeth* can be helpful if you are finding Shakespeare's English hard to grasp, but are not really recommended otherwise as any quotations you learn for the exam must come from the original text. However, the second of these books offers both modern and the original text.

- *Macbeth The Graphic Novel: Original Text (Unabridged, British English)*, adapted by John McDonald
- *Macbeth In Plain and Simple English: A Modern Translation and the Original Version*, edited by Bookcaps

Non-fiction

- *A Preface to Shakespeare's Tragedies* by Michael Mangan

  This is a fairly academic work with some contextual information and critical analysis of *Macbeth* and other tragedies.

Useful websites

Your exam board website is a valuable resource where you can find sample exam questions and mark schemes, even sample answers like those in this guide. These resources are not just there for teachers – check out these links:

- AQA – http://aqa.org.uk/subjects/english/gcse/english-literature-8702
- Eduqas – http://eduqas.co.uk/qualifications/english-literature/gcse/
- Edexcel – http://qualifications.pearson.com/en/qualifications/edexcel-gcses/english-literature-2015.html
- OCR – www.ocr.org.uk/qualifications/gcse-english-literature-j352-from-2015/

The BBC website has many good revision materials for you to use as you prepare for your exam.

- Biographical and contextual information about Shakespeare's life and times – www.bbc.co.uk/history/people/william_shakespeare/
- Links to a range of resources, including the Bitesize revision materials, also recent clips from *Macbeth* in performance, on TV and radio – www.bbc.co.uk/search?q=macbeth

A search for video clips online will find you many extracts from stage and film productions of *Macbeth*.

- BBC animated *Macbeth* – Shakespeare's words but cut down to just under half an hour – www.dailymotion.com/video/x272nl9_shakespeare-the-animated-tales-01x03-macbeth-eng-subs_shortfilms

Answers

Answers to Review your learning questions

Context (p. 12)

1   The context of a play includes the social, historical, cultural and literary factors which influenced the author, and the ways different readers respond to the play in different times and places.

2   Few of Shakespeare's plays have plots he invented. *Macbeth* is based on a school history book, *Holinshed's Chronicles,* and Banquo was the historical ancestor of the Stewart line of kings.

3   James I of England – who had been James VI of Scotland. In 1603 his rule marked the beginning of the United Kingdom. Banquo was the historical ancestor of the Stewart line of kings.

4   Most people were devout Christians. Mainly they followed the Protestant faith, though some still secretly practised 'the old religion' of Catholicism.

5   Two reasons: first, James I was Scottish. He was not very popular at the beginning of his reign and this play aimed to please by including ideas that were of concern to him (e.g. the divine right of kings, witchcraft). Second, Shakespeare had to be sure not to offend those in power by appearing critical of English society. By setting the play in eleventh century Scotland he could raise all the questions he wanted.

6   Although a modern audience may find it difficult to make sense of some of the religious beliefs of Shakespeare's time, there are aspects which give the play timeless appeal: the supernatural in the form of witches and ghosts, themes concerning treachery and violence, Macbeth's relationship with his wife. The number of film adaptations is an indicator of the play's enduring appeal.

Plot and structure (p. 35)

1   Deaths: Macdonald, First Thane of Cawdor, Duncan, Banquo, Lady Macduff, Son of Macduff, Lady Macbeth, Young Siward, Macbeth.

2   Macduff

3   The Porter is a source of comic relief after one of the most tense scenes in the play – the murder of Duncan and the Macbeths' reaction to it. Even though his words let the audience relax and laugh, his game of being the Porter at the gates of hell still has a dark side to it.

4 She sends the guests away.

5 Because Macduff is out of reach in England.

6 The English army cut down the tree branches for camouflage as they approach Macbeth's castle.

7 The ending can be seen as the action coming full circle, so that Malcolm brings back the order to Scotland that was lost when his father was assassinated. The similarity between the end of the battles and the speeches made by the two kings is striking. (Some directors end on a less certain note – the witches are still there with the potential to cause further disruption. Look out for productions which hint that all is not as resolved as it seems.)

8 This is not simple to answer: if the witches had not put the idea of being king into Macbeth's head in the first place, the rest of the plot may never have followed. However, it is Lady Macbeth's influence that moves him from thoughts to deeds. The witches are the direct cause of the death of Macduff's entire household. There is a debate to be had about how far the forces of evil unite the witches and Lady Macbeth at some points in the play.

Characterisation (p. 49)

1 Characters can be presented by any of the following: **words** – what a character says in dialogue or soliloquy; **actions** – what a character does; **words** – what other characters say about them; **events** (and the character's involvement in them) – effects of dramatic structure.

2 There are three female characters: Lady Macbeth, Lady Macduff and the gentlewoman. But if you count the three weird sisters as women there are six in total, and if you add in Hecate and her three extra witches that makes ten.

3 King Duncan, Banquo, Macduff and Old Siward are all fathers of sons. They emphasise Macbeth's childless state and they remind us that part of being a man is to be a person capable of love for his children.

4 Duncan symbolises the power of God on earth. The witches symbolise the power of the devil. Together they relate to many themes including those of order and chaos, light and dark – and the opposition of good and evil.

5 Macbeth

6 These words are spoken by Banquo to Ross and Angus about Macbeth. They suggest the theme of appearance and reality/disguise/clothing imagery.

7 Doctor to gentlewoman describing Lady Macbeth's sleepwalking – theme sickness and health.

Themes (p. 59)

1 A theme is an idea explored by a writer.

2 The themes identified in this guide are: order and chaos, ambition, the supernatural, light and darkness, appearance and reality, sickness and health.

3 This is arguable, but appearance and reality (the whole idea of concealing the truth) or perhaps the theme of light and darkness which is associated with this.

4 The weird sisters demonstrate most consistently that appearance, and words, may be deceptive.

5 The theme most associated with historical context is order and chaos.

6 Three examples of themes linking with imagery are: light and darkness, sickness and health and the clothing imagery connected with appearance.

7 Ambition – Macbeth's fatal flaw – makes him a tragic hero.

8 This should be your own opinion but it is worth discussing with others studying the play. As above, some of the themes deriving from Christian belief may be difficult for a modern audience to grasp, but the theme of ambition and the destructive effect it can have on relationships, for example, is still relevant to an audience in the twenty-first century.

Language, style and analysis (p. 69)

1 Dialogue reveals character though the words they speak and the words spoken to and about them.

2 Soliloquies are particularly important as they are private thoughts spoken aloud by an actor alone on stage, so they are honest and therefore very revealing.

3 Prose: the porter, murderers, Lady Macduff (when distressed) and Lady Macbeth (when mad). They are mainly the lower status characters, but note that prose can also reveal an agitated state of mind. Poetry (blank verse): Macbeth, King Duncan, Lady Macbeth, Banquo, Malcolm, Macduff and all of the other noble characters who are higher in status. The witches speak in a different pattern of verse, like a chant.

4 Stichomythia is a technique where ten-syllable lines of blank verse are shared between characters. It is an effective way of conveying tension.

5 Comic relief is a way of introducing crude humour, while irony is sometimes a source of dark humour.

6 There are many possibilities – see examples in this section of the guide.

7 Symbolism connected with birds of prey shows the downfall of Macbeth from a great warrior to murderous tyrant.

8 Dramatic irony occurs when the audience knows something the characters on stage are not aware of. See examples on pp. 68–69.

Tackling the exams (p. 78)

1 Paper 1 for AQA, Edexcel and Eduqas. Paper 2 for OCR.

2 No.

3 Only if you are sitting the OCR exam.

4 Between 45 and 55 minutes for AQA, Edexcel and OCR. One hour for Eduqas, which has a two-part question with a 20 minute/40 minute split.

5 Quotations are a good way of supporting a point. They need not be long, and ideally should be embedded in your writing.

6 Yes, unless you are sitting the Edexcel exam.

7 A plan will help you to organise your thoughts and avoid a muddle.

8 Check your work to make sure you have done your very best.

Assessment Objectives and skills (p. 83)

1 There are four Assessment Objectives.

2 AO1 assesses your understanding of the text and your ability to support your ideas with evidence.

3 AO2 requires comment about how the writer uses language, form and structure to create effects.

4 AO3 refers to the relationship between texts and the contexts in which they were written.

5 AO4 refers to the accuracy of spelling, punctuation and grammar. AQA, Eduqas and OCR give marks for AO4.

6 All four exam boards give marks for AO1, AO2 and AO3. AO3 has the least number of marks. AO2 is important – you need to check how many marks your board gives to this AO.

7 Do not: re-tell the story, quote at length, identify devices without explaining their effects, offer unsupported opinions, or write about characters as if they are real.